**Class, Culture
and the Curriculum**

STUDENTS LIBRARY OF EDUCATION

Class, Culture
and the Curriculum

Denis Lawton

Institute of Education
University of London

Routledge & Kegan Paul

London and Boston

First published in 1975
by Routledge & Kegan Paul Ltd
Broadway House, 68-74 Carter Lane,
London EC4V 5EL and
9 Park Street,
Boston, Mass. 02108, USA
Set in 10 point Pilgrim on 11 point body
and printed in Great Britain by
Northumberland Press Ltd, Gateshead

ISBN 0 7100 8053 0 (c)
       0 7100 8054 9 (p)

THE STUDENTS LIBRARY OF EDUCATION has been designed to meet the needs of students of Education at Colleges of Education and at University Institutes and Departments. It will also be valuable for practising teachers and educationists. The series takes full account of the latest developments in teacher-training and of new methods and approaches in education. Separate volumes will provide authorative and up-to-date accounts of the topics within the major fields of sociology, philosophy and history of education, educational psychology, and method. Care has been taken that specialist topics are treated lucidly and usefully for the non-specialist reader. Altogether, the Students Library of Education will provide a comprehensive introduction and guide to anyone concerned with the study of education, and with educational theory and practice.

The literature of education contains a great deal on the teaching of individual subjects, but less by way of systematic description and analysis of the whole curriculum, its principles of organization and the social, political and epistemological assumptions that underly its structure and content. We are now beginning to achieve a much better understanding of the implications of a common or differentiated curriculum for children of different ages and measured abilities, and of the difficulties that must be faced in tackling problems of curriculum change. Denis Lawton has already made a substantial contribution to this understanding in his *Social Class, Language and Education* (Routledge, 1968) and in other publications concerned with the social studies. *Class, Culture and the Curriculum* argues the case for a genuinely common curriculum, rooted in the organization of human knowledge. At a time when the debate on equality, opportunity and the organization of teaching and learning is assuming a new and sharper form, his book will be of great value for students pursuing courses in curriculum studies and the sociology of education.

WILLIAM TAYLOR

Contents

Acknowledgments   ix

1 Introduction: the two traditions of schooling and
   curriculum   1
   Nineteenth-century heritage   1
   The 1944 Education Act   3
   Development of the equality ideal   3
   Definitions of curriculum   6
   Progressives, idealists and the curriculum   7
   Summary   8

2 The meaning of culture   9
   Definitions of culture   9
   Three views of culture and education   11
   Bantock   11
   Hirst   16
   Williams   19
   Summary   25

3 Social class and culture   27
   Social class and equality of opportunity in education   27
   Cultural relativism   28
   The meaning of social class   29
   Thompson: 'The Making of the English Working Class'   31
   The culture of poverty   41
   Class and cultural differences   43
   Class and reading   45
   Class-consciousness: common culture   47
   Class and educational policy   49
   Summary   51

CONTENTS

Reed

4 Sociology, knowledge and the curriculum   52
   Marx   52
   Mannheim   53
   Berger and Luckman   55
   Young   56
   Normative and interpretive paradigms   57
   Summary   69

5 Knowledge and curriculum planning   70
   Schools and the transmission of knowledge   70
   Knowledge and the disciplines   71
   How many disciplines?   78
   Summary   82

6 A common culture curriculum   83
   Disciplines: public forms of knowledge   83
   Disciplines but not subjects   83
   Curriculum planning: five stages of selection   85
   Coverage and balance   87
   J. White: a compulsory curriculum?   90
   Summary   97

7 Common culture curricula in three schools   99
   Sheredes School   100
   Thomas Calton School   103
   Chatham South School   107
   Discussion   108

8 Summary and conclusion : social justice and education   113

   Suggestions for further reading   118

   Bibliography   119

Acknowledgments

I should like to thank two or three generations of M.A. students who have discussed various aspects of this book and made me clarify my thinking on the general relation between culture and education. I am also indebted to my colleagues Peter Gordon and Richard Pring who commented on earlier drafts, and to Mr D. Foskett and Mr A. Taylor for the help they have given in the section on use of libraries in Chapter 3. Finally, I am particularly grateful to Dr William Taylor, Director of the University Institute of Education, who first suggested that I should write this book and who has given valuable advice at various stages.

D.L.

I

Introduction: the two traditions of schooling and curriculum

Nineteenth-century heritage

It is fashionable today to play down the importance of the 1944 Education Act, even to see it as part of a subtle plot to deprive the working-class of real education. In my opinion this is mistaken: in spirit the Act was a move away from an élitist view of education to a more egalitarian position; in law it established the principle of free compulsory secondary education for *all* young people up to the age of sixteen.

This was clearly a major turning-point in English education, and in order to appreciate its full importance it will be necessary from time to time in this book to look back to the nineteenth century. Throughout the nineteenth century there were two quite distinct traditions of schooling which developed along very different lines and established two distinct kinds of curricula which were not only different but contained aims and assumptions which hardly ever overlapped or even came close to each other. On the one hand there was the public school/grammar school tradition of education for leadership, which gave rise to a curriculum for 'Christian gentlemen' who would become the leaders of society—managers in industry at home, or district officers in the colonies. Those who were to fill such roles were seen as needing a particular kind of character training, and secondly, the kind of knowledge which would be an obvious badge of their exclusive rank. For this purpose it was appropriate that the curriculum be based upon the classical foundations provided by Greek and Latin.

On the other hand the elementary school tradition was especially intended to train the 'lower orders'. Elementary schools were designed to produce a labour force able to understand simple written instructions and capable of making elementary calculations —the skills necessary for a competent factory labour force. It was also important that the pupils should be trained to be obedient and to have respect for the property of their betters. Throughout the nineteenth century there was a struggle to make sure that elementary education would not give the lower orders ideas above their station. The curriculum of elementary schools consisted of reading, writing and ciphering. At the beginning, even writing was regarded as potentially dangerous. Early advocates of elementary education, such as Hannah Moore or Patrick Colquhoun, were often anxious to reassure the middle classes that elementary education would not be *too* good (Colquhoun, 1806; quoted by Altick 1957, p. 143):

It is not proposed that the children of the poor should be educated in a manner to elevate their minds above the rank they are destined to fill in society.... Utopian schemes for an extensive diffusion of knowledge would be injurious and absurd.

Neither of these two kinds of education or schooling remained static in the nineteenth century, and as upper elementary teaching developed, it sometimes came very close to being 'secondary'. Again, some thought that this was becoming dangerously similar to the education of the middle classes, and successful attempts were made to nip such developments in the bud. For example, in the last quarter of the nineteenth century the London School Board was allowing education which went far beyond what was regarded as 'elementary' by most people interested in education at the time. A dispute eventually arose about the appropriateness of such expenditure out of the rates, and as a result of a legal action (known as the Cockerton Case after the name of the auditor) judgment was given against the London School Board in 1899. The statement of Mr Justice Mills, who presided, is very interesting. He unequivocally condemned the London developments and stated that the notion that School Boards were 'free to teach at the expense of the ratepayers to adults and children indiscriminately the higher mathematics, advanced chemistry both theoretical and practical, political economy, art of a kind wholly beyond anything that can be taught to children, French, German, history and I know not what, appears to me to be the *ne plus ultra* of extravagance' (quoted by Armytage, 1964, p. 185). Thus the attempt of one progressive School Board to give children 'secondary' education under the guise of elementary education had been declared illegal. After 1902 such subterfuge as had been practised by London was not necessary, since the Balfour Act allowed the setting up of local county grammar schools. But only a small proportion of working-class children ever reached grammar schools and, for the vast majority of the population, until 1944 the 'right' kind of education was elementary.

The 1944 Education Act

For these reasons the 1944 Education Act should be seen as evidence of a dramatic change in attitude. The fundamental change was that two traditions—secondary and elementary—*could* now become one tradition: the principle of equality of opportunity was established even if the realization was still extremely difficult.

It is not, however, altogether surprising that the reaction of many people to the 1944 Education Act, including that of some prominent educationists, was to continue to think in terms of the two traditions and to develop secondary modern schools for about 75 per cent of the eleven to fifteen age group, very much as an extension of the elementary school tradition. This trend had been foreshadowed by official government reports such as the Spens Report 1938 and the Norwood Report 1943 which had established a convenient doctrine of there being three different kinds of ability which required different kinds of secondary schools. Thus the major reform of providing real secondary education for all pupils, which might be assumed to be implicit in the 1944 Act, was watered down into the policy of tripartite secondary education— different kinds of schools and curricula, to match levels of measured ability. It has taken some time to revert to a consideration of the possibility of common schools with common curricula for all pupils.

Development of the equality ideal

A simplified history of education in the twentieth century might therefore be divided into the following stages:

Stage 1 In the 1920s and 1930s there was some pressure to achieve greater access to secondary education for larger numbers of working-class pupils, i.e. this was a meritocratic, rather than an egalitarian, stage concerned with fairer selection rather than equality.

Stage 2 Roughly the 1940s and 1950s: growth of secondary education for all in the diluted form of a tripartite system; then the gradual realization that the tripartite system was unworkable and unjust. Technical schools (the second division of the tripartite system) simply did not develop in most parts of the country. The system was soon effectively bipartite rather than tripartite: grammar schools for roughly the top 20 per cent of the ability

3

range and secondary modern schools for the rest, who were inevitably seen as non-academic or less able. Furthermore, there were enormous regional differences in grammar school places, which could not be justified on any grounds and which made the system appear to be very unfair. The policy of parity of esteem— that is, the notion that grammar and secondary modern schools should be seen as different but equal—was never, as Olive Banks (1955) pointed out, a realistic possibility in a society where differences in prestige were so closely connected with occupation, and occupational placement was so closely connected with educational achievement.

Stage 3 The 1960s: the growth of comprehensive schools— common secondary schools theoretically presenting equal educational opportunity or equally fair chances for all pupils but which were far from successful in practice. Julienne Ford (1969) and others, pointed out that if comprehensive schools simply operated a tripartite system under one roof, very little was gained by abolishing selection at 11+. Young and Armstrong (1965) had already written about alternative methods of comprehensive organization, moving away from selection and streaming.

Stage 4 The 1970s: an increase of interest in questions about the secondary *curriculum*. For example, 'What is the point of common schools without a common curriculum?' 'How can we have genuine comprehensive education unless schools transmit a common culture?'

Up to this time the problems had been seen almost exclusively in terms of the structure and organization of secondary schools, but by now it was apparent that such questions had to be considered in conjunction with the content of the curriculum. Even the most 'progressive' comprehensive schools had tended to operate with a watered-down version of a grammar school curriculum or an uneasy amalgamation of elementary and grammar curricula. Very few comprehensive schools had thought out their curriculum from first principles.

I do not here wish to review the arguments for and against comprehensive schools (a useful summary is contained in Ford, 1969, Chapter 1); nor would it be useful to trace in detail the historical development of the gradual if uncertain move towards a comprehensive secondary system (see Parkinson, 1970, or Lawton, 1973). The whole question of comprehensive schools is sometimes treated as a simple political battle with the Labour Party supporting the comprehensive ideal and the Conservatives resisting. The reality is much more complicated than that. First of all it has to be remembered that for a number of years the Conservative Party has been officially committed to support some kind of comprehensive plans in some areas; and on the Labour Party side there has been much confusion about what 'comprehensive' really means; and as Parkinson (1970) has shown, Labour Party policy has often resulted in a view of comprehensive education expressed in meritocratic rather than egalitarian terms, concentrating on better opportunities to become unequal rather than on equality. In so far as one can generalize about the two parties' views on secondary education it is still probably more correct to see the differences in the way Parkinson (1970, p. 21) described the two positions during the 1930s: 'Basically, the Conservative Government retained a very élitist notion of education, subscribing to the concept of an educational ladder as opposed to the "broad highway" of the Labour Party.'

In some ways it is easier to grasp the notion of the ladder than the 'broad highway'—the nature of the highway and even its general direction lack clarity, and has only been examined in terms of curriculum content during the last few years. In this book, I want to accept the existence and growth in the number of comprehensive schools, and also to accept the evidence of such researchers as Benn and Simon (1970) who have demonstrated that not only is the number of comprehensive schools increasing, but also that comprehensive schools are now tending to move away from meritocratic to more egalitarian positions. In other words, more and more comprehensive schools are abolishing selection and streaming in the early years and wish to preserve mixed-ability groups and a common curriculum for as long as possible.

The problems that I wish to examine are those arising out of this egalitarian trend. There are many practical problems of teaching-methods and organization for mixed-ability groups, but there are also fundamental theoretical questions about curriculum that teachers and schools cannot escape. If comprehensive schools are now really trying to plan a curriculum which is suitable for all pupils—a common curriculum—it is necessary to find some theoretical basis for such a plan. One view is that a common curriculum must be derived from a common culture. But this in turn raises other difficult issues. What is meant by a common culture? Is it meaningful to talk of a common culture in a pluralistic society? Would it be better to think in terms of a variety of curricula for a multi-cultural society? Questions about the meaning of culture will be explored in Chapter 2, and the issue of a common culture and common curriculum will be discussed in the third and subsequent chapters.

Definitions of curriculum

I have already suggested that a dominant characteristic of nineteenth-century education was the existence of two kinds of schools—public/grammar and elementary—with two totally different curricular traditions. But what precisely is meant by curriculum? There are at least two views on the meaning that can be attached to the word 'curriculum'. One view which was until recently generally accepted, was that the curriculum of a school was what was officially taught in lessons. According to this view, if you wanted to know about the school curriculum you would look carefully at the timetable. This meaning of curriculum has its attractions, not least in its clarity and simplicity, but it has also led to certain kinds of confusion. Sometimes suggestions have been made (for example, in the Newsom Report) that certain extra-curricular activities were so important that they should be made compulsory for all pupils. So when does an extra-curricular activity become part of the curriculum? Is it when it appears on the time-table, or when it is compulsory, or when it can be defined as a lesson?

Another disadvantage of the very limited but precise view of 'curriculum as timetable' is that many educationists would suggest that often the most important aspects of an educational programme are *not* included in the timetable at all, and only a very naïve parent would confine his investigations of a school's curriculum to a look at the timetable. Some educationists have also been driven to inventing the term 'the hidden curriculum' to convey the idea that some school activities, such as the prefect system or the cadet corps, are very powerful and influential but would not appear on the timetable as curriculum. Thus some writers (Kerr, 1968) would want curriculum to be used in a much wider sense: 'All the learning which is planned or guided by the school, whether it is carried on in groups or individually inside or outside the school.' This much wider definition of curriculum is necessary if we are to avoid semantic arguments about whether something is curricular or extra-curricular; it also avoids the assumption that all, or at least all the important, learning takes place by means of lessons and subjects.

For the purpose of this book I should, however, like to describe the curriculum in a slightly different way. It is not in any sense opposed to Kerr's definition, but places the emphasis rather differently. It seems to me that the school curriculum (in the wider sense) is essentially *a selection from the culture of a society*. Certain aspects of our way of life, certain kinds of knowledge, certain attitudes and values are regarded as so important that their transmission to the next generation is not left to chance in our society but is entrusted to specially-trained professionals (teachers) in elaborate and expensive institutions (schools). Not everything in a culture is regarded as of such importance, and in any case, time is limited, so *selection* has to be made. Different schools may make different kinds of selection from the culture: teachers may have different lists of priorities, but all teachers and all schools make selections of some kind from the culture. I propose to use the term curriculum to cover such selections from the culture made by schools. The way in which they decide on priorities and put these priorities into practice, I would describe as curriculum planning.

Progressives, idealists and the curriculum

It has often been observed that one of the features of educational debate is the tendency for individual educationists to be put into closed, ideological categories. For example, Julia Evetts (1973) has described the polarization between 'progressives' and 'idealists' in education. Progressives are said to see education in terms of growth, to see teaching as child-centred rather than subject-centred, and to see the curriculum as an inter-disciplinary one, based on the needs and interests of the children; progressives also have views on such topics as intelligence and equality which make them advocates of comprehensive schools and non-streaming. On the other hand, idealists are supposed to see education in terms of acquiring knowledge, to see teaching in terms of initiating pupils into traditional culture, and to see the curriculum organized to transmit an understanding of established disciplines; idealists also tend to approve of selection in education and therefore to disapprove of comprehensive schools and, especially teaching in mixed-ability groups. Mrs Evetts's description of the two educational views—progressive and idealist—is an interesting and valuable one, but the argument contained in this book will provide an exception to her general rule. I welcome the growth of comprehensive schools and I see unstreaming as part of their logical development—in this I am a 'progressive'; but my definition of curriculum would seem to stamp me as an idealist, and this will be confirmed later in the book when I stress the need for a structured curriculum and the necessity for this structure not to be based simply on children's 'needs' but on knowledge. This is implicit in my definition of curriculum as a selection from culture; later in the book the necessity of the selection being structured in terms of disciplines will become explicit.

The next chapter will be concerned with a discussion of the meaning of culture, and its significance in curriculum planning.

Summary

My basic premise is that up to 1944 there were two very different kinds of selection from the culture; high-status knowledge plus a certain kind of character training for the future leaders of society, in public and grammar schools; low-status, 'elementary' practical skills, and training for obedience and conformity for the future 'lower orders'. After 1944 this simple and convenient segregation of curricula was complicated by the abolition of elementary education. Since 1944 very little thinking (and planning) has been done to answer the question 'What kind of selection from culture (or cultures) is appropriate for secondary education for all?'

2

The meaning of culture

In the last chapter, I described the curriculum as a selection from the culture of a society. The idea behind that definition was that there are some aspects of our way of life that are regarded as so valuable that their survival is not left to chance but are entrusted to teachers for expert transmission to the young. In the first part of this chapter it will be necessary to clarify what is meant by 'culture' in this context; in the second part of the chapter I want to develop the idea that the possession of different views of the culture may have important effects on attitudes towards education and curriculum. To illustrate this point I shall examine the views of three important writers on culture and education; Bantock, Hirst and Williams.

Definitions of culture

It has often been pointed out that the word 'culture' has many distinct, if overlapping, meanings. The two main ways in which the word is used are the *popular* usage, and the *technical* term 'culture' as used by anthropologists and sociologists. The popular usage tends to designate certain kinds of interests and activities such as 'highbrow' music, literature and art; ten years ago it might have been summed up by reference to the BBC Third Programme. Certainly in popular usage the word 'culture' is identified with some kind of 'high' (i.e. minority-taste) culture, and possibly also with public school or Oxbridge education. A 'cultured voice' is another phrase which used to express this view, but that phrase is also now much less in use than in former years. Thus the popular usage of 'culture' confuses some kinds of minority tastes with social position and élite education. It is precisely this confusion which in more general educational terms leads to muddled thinking about culture and curriculum planning.

Raymond Williams has examined the change in the meaning of the word in his very important book *Culture and Society 1780-1950*. Before 1780, according to Williams, 'culture' meant 'the tending of natural growth' and a process of human training. Later in the eighteenth century and in the early nineteenth century, 'culture' came to be a thing in itself rather than a process, 'a general state or habit of the mind' closely connected with the idea of human perfection. A second meaning of this period was 'the general state of intellectual development, in society as a whole'. A third meaning which developed was 'the general body of the arts', and a fourth meaning, later in the century, 'a whole way of life, material, intellectual and spiritual'. I shall have to return to Williams's discussion of culture later. Meanwhile we need to consider the more general definition of culture as used by sociologists and anthropologists which is very close to Williams's fourth meaning. In this scientific sense, culture is *everything* that exists in a society. Culture includes everything that is 'man-made': technological artifacts, skills, attitudes and values. Culture is regarded as a key concept in anthropology and sociology because it is culture which separates human beings from other animals. Humans are dominated much less by instincts and much more by their cultural inheritance—their behaviour patterns are acquired socially rather than biologically. Social scientists have been particularly concerned to avoid value-judgments in their descriptions, so they have tended to stress the idea of the whole way of life as the meaning of culture rather than a selection of the best or most important aspects of a way of life: 'Culture is more than a collection of mere isolated bits of behaviour. It is the integrated sum total of learned behaviour traits which are manifest and shared by the members of a society' (E. A. Hoebel, 'The Nature of Culture', in Shapiro, 1960); 'Culture is ... that complex whole which includes knowledge, belief, art, morals, law, custom, and any other capabilities and habits acquired by man as a member of society' Tylor, 1871).

A further anthropological point, of relevance to our discussion later, is that societies and their cultures differ considerably, not only in their technology but also in their attitudes, beliefs and values. Some anthropologists, such as Ruth Benedict (1934), have stressed the magnitude of these *differences*; others such as Clyde Kluckhohn (1962) have emphasized the similarities between cultures. But all social scientists are agreed that some important differences certainly exist. Hilda Taba (1962), for example, has pointed out that a key value transmitted to the young by North American cultures is the motivation to sell oneself and to excel, whereas in Samoa the opposite is the case: 'The culture [of Samoa] values self-minimization and non-presumptive behaviour' (Taba, p. 51).

It is also important to bear in mind that apart from very simple societies (such as pre-industrial Samoa) it is rarely possible to identify just one all-pervading culture; it is usually necessary to trace the inter-mixing of several different cultures which may fuse to some extent but also tend to survive as individual and distinct regional or ethnic sub-cultures. A classic case of the merging of many different cultures is the USA, which has developed a distinctive culture out of the successive generations of immigrants from various parts of the world, all of whom have contributed something to the general (or common) culture but have also in many cases retained their group characteristics which are different from those of other Americans. Thus it might be appropriate to refer to *sub-cultures* in the USA—such as the Polish sub-cultural groups in Chicago or the negroes in Harlem. As we shall see, there are also sub-cultures in the UK but it is not always easy to identify them as clearly as some of the American examples; it may also be the case that in England the major problem for education is not the continued existence of ethnic sub-cultures such as West Indians and Pakistanis but the emergence and continued existence of working-class sub-cultural groups.

Three views of culture and education

Thus, in a complex society such as ours there are at least two major educational problems associated with 'culture'. The first concerns the extent to which it is possible to identify a general or common culture as the basis for a selection for curriculum planning. The second problem concerns the extent to which sub-cultures or aspects of sub-cultures should be reflected in educational programmes or processes of curriculum planning ('Black Studies' is one current example both in the UK and the USA). Underlying the second of these two problems there is, of course, a whole set of other questions relating to the criteria by which such selections should be made.

Bantock

G. H. Bantock is one of the few educationists who have attempted to grapple with such problems, and in doing so he has put forward a third meaning of culture. Bantock begins *Culture, Industrialisation and Education* (1968) by differentiating carefully between the anthropological use of culture and the Matthew Arnold use of culture as 'the best that has been thought and said'. He then proceeds to steer a course between these two very different definitions (p. 2)

> In this book the word 'culture' is being used in a sense which lies between the two. I do not want to include everything in it because that would involve a number of trivialities; so it is applied selectively to important areas of human thought and action. But in itself it is not intended to imply anything about the value or quality of these activities and thoughts. In my meaning of the term, a folk song, a pop song, and a Beethoven symphony are similarly representative of culture; for music plays an important part in human affairs and all three are equally examples of music. We might want to argue, further, that some are more valuable forms of music than others, but we cannot deny that all three provide us with examples of a culture in this sense.

In some ways this third view of culture (i.e. a partially selective one) is useful for educational discussion since it provides a short cut by eliminating certain aspects of culture, in the anthropological sense, from our educational debate. But it also begs some important questions such as 'Why is music a non-trivial activity?' Bantock does not systematically ask these questions but eventually they cannot be escaped. Bantock (op. cit., p. 3) also points out that:

> Until the coming of industrialisation in this country, in the later eighteenth and nineteenth centuries, it has been possible to distinguish two broad cultures, using the word in the sense defined. There has been the culture of the upper classes based particularly on their ability to read and write. And there has been the culture of the ordinary people or 'folk', based largely on their traditions of oral communication.

In Chapter 3, I shall want to ask whether this kind of historical analysis is adequate; in particular how these two traditions originated and to what extent, if any, they still exist. It will also be necessary to examine carefully the claims of so-called folk culture, in the sense used by Bantock, and to see whether it should be seriously considered for transmission to the young by means of education. These two problems will be examined later; the main purpose of this section is simply to put forward the particular view of culture and education expressed by Bantock but shared by many others.

According to this view, then, the culture of a society such as ours can be sub-divided into high and low, upper-class and folk. They might both be categorized under the same headings, at least to some extent, such as music, art, etc., but they are essentially different (despite Bantock's reference to T. S. Eliot's view that 'Fine art is the refinement, not the antithesis, of popular art'). The most important difference between these two cultures is the non-literary, oral tradition of folk culture, and Bantock quotes with sympathy D. H. Lawrence's views about the essentially non-literary elements in working-class culture. According to Bantock, public or mass education has so far been a dismal failure, and this is largely because we have attempted to force a literary culture down the throats of the masses whose tradition is an oral one.

In some respects there is an evident similarity between Bantock and the once influential views of T. S. Eliot. Eliot, in his *Notes Towards The Definition of Culture* (1948), clearly identified the most worthwhile aspects of culture with the existence of a small, governing, leisured class. This class, according to Eliot, was necessary in order to create and preserve the 'high' cultural heritage and also to ensure its transmission to the next generation of that class. The hereditary element was seen to be very important and Eliot was concerned about the threat to the existence of a cultured upper-class, either by the growth of a meritocratic élite or by 'equalitarianism'. Eliot seemed to find the idea of a common culture distasteful, or even necessarily a contradiction in terms—diffusion of the precious cultural commodity among large numbers could only be a dilution of quality.

Bantock shares Eliot's disbelief in the desirability of a common culture but argues the case with closer reference to educational practice in a way that merits careful examination. The conclusion Bantock draws from his analysis is that there should be two kinds of curriculum: a high-culture curriculum for a small minority who are academically minded (drawn, presumably, largely from the upper and middle classes, whose tradition is high culture), and a totally different 'non-literary' curriculum for the masses.

Bantock has outlined his case for a non-literary curriculum in two interesting articles in the *Times Educational Supplement* which have been reprinted in Hooper (1971). Bantock's argument runs as follows: the Industrial Revolution has produced two educational problems concerning curriculum. The first of these concerns establishing a suitable curriculum for the meritocracy, to replace the classics-based curriculum thought suitable for the landed élite. The second problem concerns finding a suitable and satisfying curriculum for the majority (since the watered-down, academic curriculum has failed). Bantock mainly concerns himself with the second of these problems; I have mentioned the first problem as well, since it seems to me to be of some interest and importance.

In seeking support for his view that the majority of the population is not suited for the traditional academic curriculum, Bantock refers to a number of claims, including that of D. H. Lawrence, that a characteristic of the 'primitive mind' is that it finds difficulty in dealing with universals and is most at home with particulars; the implication is that the life tradition of working-class people is dynamic and instinctive but not truly rational. One difficulty about Bantock's argument is whether he regards this working-class and primitive response to reality simply as different from the high culture or as inferior.

Bantock goes on to quote such evidence as Bernstein's work on language to support his view that working-class children, or 'the masses', have a tradition which is not really suited to academic secondary education. Finally, Bantock brings in the psychological views of Burt, Eysenck and Jensen to stress the importance of heredity in the distribution of intelligence. He quotes as of particular importance the views of Jensen that there may be two kinds of mental functioning, 'one at the conceptual level and one at what he has termed "the level of associative learning"'. The evidence that Bantock presents to support his thesis is, however, extremely thin and of a highly controversial nature even among psychologists. It certainly could not be assumed that Bantock has demonstrated his point of view by means of the evidence that he has selected. The argument about one culture or two will be examined from a social-historical standpoint in Chapter 3.

In his outline of an alternative curriculum for the mass of the population, Bantock suggests that it should have the following characteristics: the curriculum should be aimed at practical common life; it should be concrete and specific rather than abstract; it should include aspects of television, film and popular Press; the education of the emotions should not be neglected as it is in conventional education; and finally, education should be concerned with preparation for leisure. Thus education should be liberal education but avoiding the usual concentration on reading: Bantock urges that dance and drama, and art and craft should be developed in a suitable way for working-class children.

There is much to be commended in some of Bantock's suggestions: a selection from contemporary culture (rather than past culture) would certainly include film and television studies, for example. But the question that arises immediately is 'Why is all this relevant for the masses of the population but *not* for the academic?' Do they not need to be educated emotionally? Do they not need preparation for leisure? Will not television and film and the Press be an important part of their lives as well as of the lives of the masses?

There are many other difficulties connected with Bantock's suggestions: for example, who will select the pupils for academic or for mass education? He has suggested that most of the mass-educated will be working-class in background, but who will sort out the exceptions? What about the D. H. Lawrences? It is also perhaps a little naïve to expect all members of the upper and middle classes to be academic and literary-minded. Such practical questions as these cannot be ignored in a curriculum proposal of such importance as Bantock's. Bantock's analysis of the problem is much stronger than his solution of it, although to be fair we should remember that the title of his article was 'Towards a Theory of Popular Education' (italics mine).

The most important criticism of Bantock's ideas about 'popular education', however, is that they rest on an assumption that it is possible to divide 'culture' neatly into 'high' and 'low', and also that it is possible to allocate individual human beings or groups of human beings to these two rigid categories. The reality is, I suggest, much more complex: the distinction between high and mass culture is difficult to maintain consistently, and there is a great deal of overlap, especially since television has become an important medium in nearly every household, and film has developed as an art form. Moreover, individuals may have 'highbrow' tastes in, say, music but not in literature. What Bantock has put forward as popular education could much more appropriately be regarded as part of everyone's education. As one important part of a common curriculum it would be an improvement, but as the whole of a curriculum for one section of the community it would be reactionary. John White (1973) has pointed out the similarity between Bantock's ideas for educating the 'children of the folk' and Plato's prescriptions for the 'children of bronze' whose training was quite different from the rational education of the 'children of gold'.

The real problem has been analysed in a more sensitive way by Lawrence Stenhouse in *Culture and Education* (1967, pp. 10-11). Stenhouse would agree with Bantock to some extent but his solution is quite different:

Compulsory education has provided for the majority of our people an impoverished literacy which does not support an effective culture. An academic few, who have enjoyed higher education, have entered into a culture fed by literature and the arts, but most people have not been enriched by their education to the extent we might have hoped. They have learned the basic skills of reading and writing, but they have not been taught to bend these skills to their own purposes and to make them serve their needs by introducing an element of creativity into their everyday living. In the old schoolmaster's phrase, they have 'mastered their letters'; but they have not gone on

15

to enter into the spirit of humane letters. Part of the difficulty is that it is the *spirit* of humane letters that must be conveyed, not the academic tradition of literae humaniores. As Richard Hoggart has said, 'It seems unlikely at any time, and is certainly not likely in any period which those of us now alive are likely to know, that a majority in any class will have strongly intellectual pursuits.' But he adds: 'There are other ways of being in the truth.'

Two important points emerge from this: first that there are ways other than the 'literary/academic' of being 'in the truth', and secondly that this is *not* simply a working-class problem but one which applies to a *majority* of all classes. The problem in terms of curriculum is thus to find a way of bridging the gap between the academic and the everyday, and not to force half-digested academic ideas down unwilling throats of *all* classes and all abilities: the solution does not lie in dividing people neatly into two closed categories. Bantock's main fault consists of an inadequate analysis of culture, and especially that part of culture referred to as worthwhile knowledge. Bantock may be right in suggesting that compulsory education has failed. But if so it has failed for all classes, not just working-class children.

Hirst

One of the curriculum theorists whose views were referred to but rejected by Bantock was P. H. Hirst. Hirst's views on the relationship between culture and curriculum are summarized below but should be read carefully in one of the original sources. Bantock's major disagreement with Hirst concerns the suggestion that there is no need for a 'radically new pattern of the curriculum'. Bantock cannot accept Hirst's view that 'the central objectives of education are development of mind', or that:

> no matter what the ability of the child may be, the heart of all his development as a rational being is, I am saying, intellectual. Maybe we shall need very special methods to achieve this development in some cases. Maybe we have still to find the best methods for the majority of people. But let us never lose sight of the intellectual aim upon which so much else, nearly everything else, depends. Secondly, it seems to me that we must get away completely from the idea that linguistic and abstract forms of thought are not for some people.
> (Schools Council, *Working Paper No. 12: 'The Educational Implications of Social and Economic Change'*, quoted by Bantock (1971, p. 257).

16

Hirst does not talk in terms of curriculum as a selection from the culture, and I may be doing less than justice to his thesis by trying to force it into my own framework, but the theory seems to me to run as follows: the first principle is that we should be clear about our educational goals. The second is that 'the central objectives of education are developments of mind'. Hirst sees the development of mind in terms of the development of 'forms of knowledge' (Hirst and Peters, 1970, pp. 63-4):

Detailed studies suggest that some seven areas can be distinguished, each of which necessarily involves the use of concepts of a particular kind and a distinctive type of test for its objective claims. The truths of:

1. *Formal logic and mathematics* involve concepts that pick out relations of a general abstract kind; their deducibility within an axiom system is the particular test for truth.
2. *The physical sciences* on the other hand, are concerned with truths that, in the last analysis, stand or fall by the tests of observation by the senses. Abstract though the theoretical concepts they employ may be, the sciences necessarily employ concepts for what is seen, heard, felt, touched or smelt; for it is with an understanding and knowledge of the sensible world that they are concerned.
3. To be clearly distinguished from knowledge and experience of the physical world is our *awareness and understanding of our own and other people's minds*. Concepts like those of 'believing', 'deciding', 'intending', 'wanting', 'acting', 'hoping', and 'enjoying', which are essential to inter-personal experience and knowledge, do not pick out, in any straightforward way what is observable by the senses. Indeed the phrase 'knowledge without observation' has been coined to make this point. The precise nature of the grounds of our objective judgments in this area is not yet adequately understood, though their irreducibility to other types of test can perhaps be most readily seen in judgments of our own states of mind.
4. *Moral judgment and awareness* necessitate, in their turn, another family of concepts such as 'ought', 'wrong', and 'duty'. Unless actions or states are understood in such terms, it is not their moral character of which we are aware. The claim to objectivity in the case of moral judgments is a matter of long standing dispute, but the sustained attempts that have been made to show the objectivity of morals, and its irreducibility to other forms of knowledge, make this domain one which must be recognised

17

as having serious claims to independent status.

5. Likewise the claims for a distinctive mode of objective *aesthetic experience*, using forms of expression not confined to the linguistic, must be taken seriously, even though much philosophical work remains to be done.

6. *Religious* claims in their traditional forms certainly make use of concepts which, it is now maintained, are irreducible in character. Whether or not there are objective grounds for what is asserted is again a matter on which more has yet to be said. The case would certainly seem to be one that cannot be simply dismissed.

7. Finally, philosophical understanding as indicated in chapter 1 would seem to involve unique second order concepts and forms of objective tests irreducible to those of any first order kind.

This passage from Hirst and Peters could well stimulate a variety of discussions about the nature of curriculum planning; many educationists such as Stenhouse (1973) and Eisner (1969) would have serious doubts about the clear-cut nature of specifiable objectives, for example. I have included Hirst's viewpoint here as an example of curriculum planning which is largely 'non-cultural' in the sense of being transcultural. This is because Hirst sees the curriculum largely in terms of knowledge, and the structure and organization of knowledge is, by his analysis, universal rather than culturally based. For this reason Hirst will have no truck with different kinds of curriculum for different levels of ability, or different areas, or different sub-cultural interests. The main objectives of education are concerned with knowledge; most school knowledge should not be bound to specific sub-cultures—it is objective and universal; therefore if we are serious in our desire to educate everyone in a society, then everyone must have access to the same kinds of knowledge. Everyone needs the same kind of curriculum (although, of course, different methods of attaining the curriculum objectives might well be employed): the ends will be the same but the means may differ. For Hirst, then, the traditional secondary curriculum, with some important modifications such as the inclusion of social sciences and moral education, will provide the appropriate selection from the culture for all pupils. The question of the sub-cultural background of the pupils is irrelevant to the *ends* (or goals) of education, but may be very relevant to the *means* (i.e. teaching method and content). A similar conclusion is reached by John White in his recent book *Towards a Compulsory Curriculum* (1973). White accepts Hirst's basic thesis, as outlined above, but develops the forms of knowledge into a curriculum subdivided into what should be compulsory and what should be offered as optional experiences. Further reference to this book will be made in Chapter 6.

Williams

As a final example of a theorist with views on the relation between culture and education, I should like to look at the work of Raymond Williams. Williams's ideas can be seen mainly in two important books: *Culture and Education* (1958) and *The Long Revolution* (1961). (A different kind of insight into the problem can also be gained from his novel *Border Country*.) In particular, the first chapter of Part 2 of *The Long Revolution*, 'Education and British Society', should be read carefully by all interested in this question. Williams begins his chapter on education and British society with this statement (p. 145):

> There are clear and obvious connections between the quality of a culture and the quality of its system of education. In our time we have settled to saying that the improvement of our culture is a matter of improving and extending our national education, and in one sense this is obviously true.

One interesting point about this introductory remark is that although Williams is using the word 'culture' in its anthropological sense he does not adopt the extreme social science relativist position of pretending that all cultures are equally valuable or equally worthwhile. This is a very important point to be made at the beginning of his argument.

Williams also suggests that we cannot discuss the relation between culture and education adequately without historical analysis —the past is contained in the present. As part of his analysis Williams examines education systems in a general way and suggests three main aims or purposes:

1. To pass on the accepted behaviour and values of society,
2. the general knowledge and attitudes appropriate to an educated man, and
3. a particular skill by which he will earn a living.

All brief statements of educational aims are open to criticism, and this set of three may seem too simple, but Williams clearly recognizes that the three overlap and inter-relate, and also that the general pattern of culture may be subject to change, either slow or rapid; the aims are not intended to convey a static view of education and culture.

Williams's historical analysis is necessarily a partial one (op. cit., p. 147):

I propose to examine the history of English education from this particular point of view: to see the changing complex of actual relations, in social training, subjects taught, definitions of general education, in the context of a developing society.

Williams sees a close relationship between training for vocation, training to social character and training to a particular civilization. In the first English schools in the sixth century the intention was to produce priests and monks, for example. For this Latin was essential. Of necessity this kind of education was only for a few, but of course the 'few' were meant to interpret the scriptures and thus make them available to the many—thus to use the modern word 'élitist' would not be completely appropriate. Later there was an extension of the curriculum to include rhetoric and logic, but the framework was still firmly Christian. In this sense, a common Christian culture pervaded the whole of society: education was vocational, serving the needs of a Christian society. Schools were not the only educational (and vocational) institutions, however: the apprenticeship system catered for craftsmen and tradesmen, and chivalric training was provided for children of the nobility. Thus although there was a common culture, different curricular selections were made according to social rank, but there was some opportunity for social mobility, mainly by joining the ranks of the clergy.

Even after the Reformation, the central educational institution remained the grammar school, but it was no longer so closely connected with the Church. (Education was becoming 'private' rather than 'national'.) The major achievements of the Renaissance were, however, almost completely ignored by the grammar schools—education was lagging behind the changes in society; curricular change was slower than cultural change: literature in the English language, geography, painting, music, philosophy and science found no place in the grammar school curriculum.

As the population expanded and more people were concentrated in towns, education became more rigidly organized along class lines. Gradually, schools of a sort were provided for the poor, but it was training of a very limited kind. The Clarendon Report 1864, the Public Schools Act 1868, the Taunton Report 1868, the Headmasters' Conference 1869 and the Endowed Schools Act 1869 all emphasized the class nature of the structure of secondary education.

Williams argues that the two major pressures—industrial and democratic—gave rise to many kinds of arguments about the purposes of education. In particular he selects for discussion three responses to industrial and democratic developments:

1. The genuine response to the growth of *democracy* (by men such as Mill, Carlyle, Ruskin and Arnold).
2. The protective response, or *moral rescue* response, to the growth of democracy, typical of those who feared the extensions of the franchise and said, 'our future masters ... should at least learn their letters'.
3. The practical *vocational* response by those, such as Forster in 1870, who felt that only education could preserve industrial prosperity.

Williams regards both the industrial and democratic arguments as valid but suggests that an over-emphasis of the industrial argument has distorted education, particularly in the direction of training a passive work force. Such a view of education was, according to Williams, challenged from two sides during the nineteenth century: by those who believed that an essential aspect of democracy was the natural right to be educated; and also from the other side by those who might have opposed democracy but felt that man's spiritual health depended on 'liberal' or 'humane' education rather than specialized work training. Thus there were three groups in the nineteenth-century debate:

1. The public educators (who saw education as a natural right).
2. The industrial trainers (who saw education as a means of economic efficiency).
3. The old humanists (who saw education in a liberal or humane way but not as vocational training).

Williams argues that the curriculum which emerged was a compromise between all three, but with the influence of the industrial trainers predominant (op. cit., p. 163):

The significant case is the long controversy over science and technical education. If we look at the range of scientific discovery between the seventeenth and the end of the nineteenth century, it is clear that its importance lies only in part in its transformation of the techniques of production and communication: indeed lies equally in its transformation of man's view of himself and of his world. Yet the decisive educational interpretation of this new knowledge was not in terms of its essential contribution to liberal studies but in terms of technical training for a particular class of men. The old humanists muddled the issue by claiming a fundamental distinction between their traditional learning and that of the new

disciplines, and it was from this kind of thinking that there
developed the absurd defensive reaction that all real learning
was undertaken without thought of practical advantage. In
fact, as the educational history shows, the classical linguistic
disciplines were primarily vocational, but these particular
vocations had acquired a separate traditional dignity, which
was refused to vocations now of equal human relevance. Thus,
instead of the new learning broadening a general curriculum,
it was neglected, and in the end reluctantly admitted on the
grounds that it was of a purely technical kind. The pressure of
the industrial trainers eventually prevailed, though not with any
general adequacy until the Technical Instruction Act of 1889,
and even here, significantly it was instruction rather than
education.

Only exceptional men such as Huxley saw that science should
become part of general education and liberal culture, and that
there should also be specific and technical training of all kinds just
as doctors and lawyers receive professional training. But what
actually happened in the nineteenth century was an intensification
of class-thinking in education: trade and industry were relegated
to the lower classes, and successful industrialists wanted their sons
to move into the non-work world of the gentry. Important changes
in the culture did not result in corresponding changes in the content
of education.

In the twentieth century, the nineteenth-century framework has
been expanded and improved. In theory, the views of the public
educators have been accepted; but in practice the ideal has not
been realized: there is still a huge gap between 'private' and 'state'
education, both in quality and quantity. Since Williams's book was
published (1961), sociologists and official government reports have
continued to turn out statistical evidence to support this view.
Public schools continue to be important aspects of the divisive
character of English society.

Another kind of contrast between the ideal of genuine education
as a right for everyone and the reality of the present educational
scene concerns the question of ability or intelligence. Williams
complains about (pp. 167-8):

The very odd principle that has been built into modern
English education: that those who are slowest to learn should
have the shortest time in which to learn, while those who learn
quickly will be able to extend the process by as much as seven
years beyond them. This is the reality of 'equality of opportunity'
which is a very different thing from real social equality. The
truth is that while for children of a particular social class we

have a conception, however imperfect, of a required minimum of general education whatever their measured intelligence might be, we have no such conception, or a much lower conception, for the majority of those outside this class.

Williams sees this stress on intelligence, and the consequent obsession with sorting and grading in education as natural to a class society. The alternative is not only a more 'open' system of education but a 'genuinely open culture'. (See also Basil Bernstein's article 'Open Schools, Open Society', *New Society*, 14th September 1967, for an interesting extension of this argument.)

Thus Williams sees our educational problems today largely in terms of successive failures of the educational system to adjust to cultural changes—for example, at the Renaissance, the Industrial Revolution and the growth of democracy. The organization of education, the content of the curriculum, and current teaching methods are, according to Williams, in need of considerable reform. At an organizational level, Williams would not want school to continue beyond sixteen—a variety of institutions offering continuing education should after that take over the needs of an educated democracy and a common culture. Up to the age of sixteen Williams offers the following as an outline, reformed curriculum, based on his historical analysis of our culture:

I would put down the following, as the minimum to aim at for every educationally normal child.
(a) Extensive practice in the fundamental languages of English and mathematics;
(b) general knowledge of ourselves and our environment, taught at the secondary stage not as separate academic disciplines but as general knowledge drawn from the disciplines which clarify at a higher stage, i.e.,
   (i)   biology, psychology,
   (ii) social history, law and political institutions, sociology, descriptive economics, geography including actual industry and trade,
   (iii) physics and chemistry;
(c) history and criticism of literature, the visual arts, music, dramatic performance, landscape and architecture;
(d) extensive practice in democratic procedures, including meetings, negotiations, and the selection and conduct of leaders in democratic organisations. Extensive practice in the use of libraries, newspapers and magazines, radio and television programmes, and other sources of information, opinion and influence;
(e) introduction to at least one other culture, including its

language, history, geography, institutions and arts, to be given in part by visiting and exchange.'

Once again criticisms could be made relating to Williams's historical analysis and his proposed solutions. But that is not my intention here: this summary of Williams's analysis has been included as an illustration of a third, very different, view of the relation between culture and education. For Williams, economic and ideological changes in society (especially the growth of industry and democracy) have brought about cultural changes which have not yet been fully assimilated by the educational system. Moreover, Williams does not hesitate to look to the future and to suggest that the logic of the situation is such that certain further cultural changes ought to be *anticipated* by education. Williams argues that if we really want a democratic society then we will need to plan for common schools with a reformed common curriculum to replace the class-based educational organizations and divisive curricula which were inherited from the class-dominated nineteenth century. Part of the difficulty here, of course, is the wide range of meanings which can be given to 'democratic'. There are some educationists who would claim to support 'democracy' but who would disagree with Williams's prescriptions.

The importance of Williams's contribution is that whilst giving due emphasis to the importance of social class in contemporary society, and recognizing that education in this country is still dominated by class-based curricular traditions, he does not make the claim that education has to be *determined* by cultural background: if participatory democracy is to become a reality, then society and education must be changed. Education cannot effect this reform unaided, but it is not completely impotent, as others have suggested. If we want a better society we need a better system of education, and part of this requirement may well be a common curriculum selected from a common culture.

To a very limited extent all three educationists referred to above are in agreement: they all recognize the importance of the transmission of culture as the basis of education, and to some extent they identify the same aspects of our traditional culture as important—for example, art and music. But they also differ considerably in the emphasis they place on certain aspects of our culture and also the kinds of selection they would make as a basis of curriculum planning: for example, Bantock has little to say about mathematics and science, Hirst has little advice to give about the link between academic learning and the everyday world, Williams seems not to be concerned with the 'disciplines' as a basis for learning. There are also other more fundamental differences: Bantock believes in different kinds of curricula for different kinds of cultural groups; Hirst advocates a common curriculum for all, based on the recognition of the importance of forms of knowledge; Williams sees the purposes of a common curriculum as even wider, having social as well as cognitive perspectives.

None of them has attempted to describe in detail how a selection from the culture might be made and structured as a planned school curriculum.

Summary

This chapter has attempted to define culture and its relation to education. The popular usage of 'culture' as high culture has to be rejected as a useful basis of discussion for educationists since it begs too many questions; the anthropological definition of culture —as everything created by man in a society—is more useful since curriculum can then be defined as a selection of content made by educationists from the whole culture.

The second part of the chapter has dealt with the views of three important theorists whose attitudes to culture and education are very different: Bantock, Hirst and Williams. The point of taking these three examples was to illustrate the thesis that how one sees culture determines one's attitude to education and to curriculum planning.

Bantock sees culture as sharply divided into two kinds: high and low culture, or élite and mass culture, or sophisticated and popular culture. His deep-rooted concern for the preservation and development of high culture, influences his educational thinking in the direction of separate schools for the future participants in high and low culture, with quite different curricula for the two groups.

Hirst, on the other hand, tends to ignore historical and social differences in cultures and sub-cultures. He sees education largely in terms of 'culture-free' knowledge. Thus for him curriculum reform is mainly a question of making available to all pupils the traditional curriculum—suitably modified to fill in the gaps in his 'forms of knowledge'. Since, according to Hirst, the curriculum is based on knowledge, it would make no sense to have different kinds of curriculum. For Hirst, a non-academic curriculum is a contradiction in terms; the problem of different levels of ability is one of teaching method not of curriculum content.

Finally, Williams sees culture in a historical setting—in particular he examines cultural change taking place over a long period of time. His analysis also shows that educational change has not kept pace with social change and cultural change, and indeed that in his view education has taken several false turnings. Williams focuses attention on the unsuitability of a class-based nineteenth-century structure of education and divisive curricula for the needs of a democratic, industrial, twentieth-century society. His solution includes a common curriculum for all pupils, but, unlike Hirst, he does not see the traditional curriculum as providing a useful basis: the planning of a common curriculum for all pupils needs to be thought out from first principles.

3

Social class and culture

Chapter 2 was concerned in general with the relation between culture and education. One of the specific problems implicit in such a discussion was also raised: namely the extent to which it is possible to base curriculum planning on a *common* culture in a society which is pluralistic. In this country the debate is currently concerned with the desirability, and even the 'morality', of imposing the 'dominant' culture on to the majority of the population—the working-class population—whose traditions and cultural standards are, according to some, very different. This chapter will be mainly concerned with an examination of so-called working-class culture, its historical background, its recent development and contemporary characteristics. Before looking at the historical background of culture in England, however, it may be useful to outline the current debate.

Social class and equality of opportunity in education

In Chapter 1, I suggested that during the 1920s and 1930s the debate about equality of opportunity in education was primarily concerned with questions about access to education. It was established that many more working-class pupils were capable (in terms of IQ) of benefiting from grammar school and university education than were actually there. The solution was often seen simply in terms of more places being made available for working-class pupils.

In the 1940s and 1950s this kind of argument continued, but with certain significant changes: more attention was paid to problems of performance and achievement within grammar (and comprehensive) schools. The problem had not simply disappeared by making educational places available—attention also had to be paid to the 'under-achieving' pupils. Sometimes the problem was seen in terms of 'pupil deficits', i.e. something lacking in a child's

home background, but also more attention was given to the fact
that schools—especially grammar schools, but some comprehensive
schools too—were middle-class institutions transmitting middle-class
values, so maybe it was the fault of the schools rather than the
children when pupils failed. This has led, more recently still, to
discussions about the relation of class to the curriculum; for
example, is the curriculum too 'middle-class' for working-class
pupils? Is such a question meaningful? As we saw in Chapter 2,
education theorists differ in their answers to this kind of question.
Bantock would presumably say that the school curriculum is too
literary and abstract for working-class pupils, who should have
something closer to their own kinds of concrete reality. On the
other hand, Hirst might dismiss class from the discussion altogether,
on the grounds that forms of knowledge are classless and that the
traditional curriculum does not need *radical* change, only a few
adjustments. Williams disagrees with both and has proposed a
different kind of curriculum for *all* pupils. Recently, a fourth view
has emerged which seems to be suggesting that the traditional curriculum has been rejected by working-class pupils because it is irrelevant to them in their environment, and that a new curriculum
should be worked out, more in keeping with working-class
traditions, concerns and interests (Midwinter, 1972, p. 13):

> The educational servicing of a multi-various society with
> a singular system leads to schools which fail to relate to the
> experience of their pupils and their catchment area. Often,
> it would appear, the curriculum is irrelevant to the community,
> its children and both their needs.

In some respects I find myself very much in sympathy with this
view, but the question of relevance is very complex and begs a
number of questions such as 'Relevant to what?' There is also the
point that *if* an environment is an extremely limiting one, then to
base the whole curriculum on 'relevance' to it may be to 'sell the
children short' in a dangerous way. Clearly this is not Midwinter's
intention but it may be the result, and if it is, it could be due to
ignoring important questions about the quality of life in certain
kinds of urban, working-class sub-cultures, as well as important
questions about the nature of knowledge.

Cultural relativism

Midwinter appears to be supporting the extreme relativist position
which is fashionable in some quarters today. He seems to be
saying that any sub-cultural values, attitudes and activities are just
as good as any others—they are different but equal. This is in

conflict with Williams's view quoted in Chapter 2 that some cultures are of a better quality than others. The extreme relativist point of view is a very difficult one to maintain consistently, however. Was the quality of life in ancient Athens really not superior to that in Sparta? Is the quality of life now in the Republic of South Africa really different but no worse than in Tanzania? As Ginsberg has pointed out in his essay 'On the Diversity of Morals' in *Essays in Sociology and Social Philosophy* (p. 236):

> the attack on humanitarian values made by the Nazis has made the doctrine of ethical relativity, adopted more or less un-reflectively by many anthropologists, emotionally untenable and has forced them ... to examine their attitude to ethical problems afresh. Like other relativists they have to face the questions whether it can really be the case that there is no rational way of deciding between the ethics of a Roosevelt and the ethics of a Hitler, and whether the moral indignation aroused by Nazi atrocities can really be intellectually on the same level as the contempt which the Nazis felt for what to them seemed the maudlin sentimentality of their opponents.

Similarly, Popper (1966) has forcefully made the point that to say that social rules or moral norms or aesthetic criteria are man-made does not necessarily lead us to the conclusion that they are completely arbitrary.

If we then accept the validity of comparing cultures and sub-cultural behaviour in terms of *quality*, we have to look at some very awkward questions indeed: for example, assuming that there is a distinct British working-class culture, what does it mean to speak of it as different from, but just as good as, middle-class and upper-class culture? Or has working-class culture in some respects been mutilated or damaged by historical events from which it has not yet recovered?

These are not purely academic questions. It is often suggested by educationists such as Brian Jackson and Eric Midwinter that schools should help to preserve the best of working-class culture, but very few positive suggestions are offered as to the qualities of this culture.

The meaning of social class

Before enquiring into the nature of social class differences it may be advisable to attempt a definition of what is meant by social class in this context. Many sociologists would assert that *stratification* of some kind exists (and has existed) in most societies, i.e. that societies can be divided into layers or ranks; some (for example,

Mayer, 1955) have suggested that it is useful to classify stratification into three 'ideal types' : caste, estate, and social class. Caste is the most rigid form of stratification, i.e. mobility from one level in society to another is extremely difficult, if not theoretically impossible : individuals are born into a position in the hierarchy; roles are ascribed rather than achieved; and caste is frequently justified by religious beliefs. Secondly, estate systems of stratification; in these societies, rank is associated with land tenure; the medieval English feudal system was a good example—land was held in return for duties owed to a feudal superior; those with little or no land were at the bottom of the hierarchy. Finally, social class is the system of stratification typical of modern industrial societies. One of the characteristics of social class is that its basis is primarily economic, i.e. it depends upon the possession of certain kinds of wealth and income; classes are not *clearly* distinct from each other —the boundaries between them are very vague; classes (unlike feudal ranks) are not legal distinctions—in theory all are equal before the law; interclass mobility is an essential feature of class (so it cannot be argued that we are a classless society because some can rise from rags to riches). Thus it might be said that Britain is a stratified society and its basic form of stratification is social class with vestigial remains of feudalism.

Many definitions of class owe something to Marx (although he was by no means the first to use the term—see Asa Briggs's essay 'The language of class in early 19th century England' in Briggs and Saville, 1967). For Marx, class was economically based, i.e. an individual's class was defined in terms of his relationship to the means of production. The owners of capital (the bourgeoisie) also possessed political power; the non-owners (the proletariat) had no political power. According to many interpretations of Marx the economic sub-structure (i.e. ownership or non-ownership of capital) determines the political and cultural superstructure. What Marx actually meant by this is often disputed but Weber was unwilling to accept this simple Marxist view and proposed an alternative, more complex thesis. Weber asserted that there are three factors involved in class : not only the *economic* factor of wealth, income and related 'life-chances', but also *status* and *power*. Status or prestige or 'social honour' was seen by Weber as a pre-capitalist feature which was still of great importance : high prestige or status does not automatically follow the possession of wealth; one's 'life-style' was also important—how money is spent, for example, as well as other aspects of normative behaviour. Finally there is the question of power or control over others; Weber, unlike Marx, did not feel that this followed automatically from the possession of wealth—there might be a high correlation between the three factors, but the relationship was a complex one.

Most contemporary discussion of social class owes a good deal to the writings of Marx and Weber. Social class, however defined, is found to be statistically related to life-chances such as infant mortality rates, and to aspects of life-style such as leisure pursuits. But three points should be stressed at this stage: although most sociologists agree that social class is very complex, in surveys people are often categorized on the single factor of occupation (or even into manual and non-manual occupations); secondly, there is rarely, if ever, a one-to-one relationship between class and any aspect of life-style or life-chances, however high the statistical correlation may be; thirdly, it is often important to distinguish between 'objective' and 'subjective' social class—a person might be clearly working-class by any defined criterion, but if he thinks of himself as middle-class, this is likely to influence his behaviour (for example, voting and life-style) in a very powerful way.

Thus, to discuss class in a meaningful way involves more than knowledge of occupation or income. Class is also complicated by the events of history: one can have very little real understanding of class and class-consciousness in Britain without an appreciation of the eighteenth- and nineteenth-century events which produced our class structure. For this reason, I want to try to review briefly some of the historical studies which might contribute to our understanding of the importance of class in our society today.

Thompson: 'The Making of the English Working Class'

An indispensable book for all serious students of this topic is Edward Thompson's *The Making of the English Working Class*. Thompson begins his preface with the following description of class:

> By class I understand a historical phenomenon, unifying a number of disparate and seemingly unconnected events, both in the raw material of experience and in consciousness. I emphasize that it is a *historical* phenomenon. I do not see class as a 'structure', nor even as a 'category', but as something which in fact happens (and can be shown to have happened) in human relationships.
>
> More than this, the notion of class entails the notion of historical relationship. Like any other relationship, it is a fluency which evades analysis if we attempt to stop it dead at any given moment and anatomize its structure. The finest-meshed sociological net cannot give us a pure specimen of class, any more than it can give us one of deference or of love. The relationship

must always be embodied in real people and in a real context. Moreover, we cannot have two distinct classes, each with an independent being, and then bring them *into* relationship with each other. We cannot have love without lovers, nor deference without squires and labourers. And class happens when some men, as a result of common experiences (inherited or shared), feel and articulate the identity of their interests as between themselves, and as against other men whose interests are different from (and usually opposed to) theirs. The class experience is largely determined by the productive relations into which men are born—or enter involuntarily. Class-consciousness is the way in which these experiences are handled in cultural terms: embodied in traditions, value-systems, ideas and institutional forms. If the experience appears as determined, class-consciousness does not. We can see a *logic* in the responses of similar occupational groups undergoing similar experiences, but we cannot predicate any *law*. Consciousness of class arises in the same way in different times and places, but never in *just* the same way.

The class system in England is one of the products of the Industrial Revolution. This does not, of course, mean that before the Industrial Revolution there was no stratification—far from it. There was a very complex ranking system. Peter Laslett, for example, in his book *The World We Have Lost*, has one chapter entitled 'A One Class Society'. The pre-industrial world in England was, in Laslett's words, 'no paradise or golden age of equality'. The family was patriarchal, so were the relationships between servant and master, lord and peasant. But life had a certain stability, warmth of personal relationships and security of duties and obligations. In order to justify his contention that pre-industrial England was a one-class society, Laslett differentiates between *class* and *status group*. A status group is a number of people banded together in the exercise of collective power, political and economic. Laslett's point seems to be that there was only one class in this sense and that those who were not members of this class were simply followers of the members of that ruling class. They had no political or economic power in any meaningful class sense.

Perhaps the most significant difference between the ruling 5 per cent and the rest of the population was that in a culture dominated by work, gentlemen did not engage in manual work. There were, therefore, vast differences in wealth, power, privilege and status, but there was only one culture, according to Laslett. Individuals played different parts within society but it was not possible to talk of sub-cultures. Rich and poor, worshipped the same God, shared beliefs and attitudes despite their differences in rank and life-style.

One important blow to this monolithic cultural system came with the Reformation. Different kinds of worship represented a serious threat to a national culture: a great deal of religious perse-cution was due as much to fear of social disunity as to religious intolerance. It seemed inconceivable that a unified nation could survive the loss of a unified Church. Religion was a very important aspect of the culture.

An even greater threat to the unified culture was to occur as a result of the Industrial Revolution. Thompson suggests that between 1780 and 1832—the crucial period of rapid social and industrial change—most English working people developed a class-conscious identity of interest which they felt to be quite different from the interests of their rulers and employers. During the same period the ruling class resolved some of their internal dissensions and 'closed ranks' in the face of an insurgent working-class. This growth of class-consciousness was so great that by 1832, according to Thomp-son, it was the most important factor in British political life.

Other writers have made much the same point as Thompson. For example, R. A. Nisbet in *The Sociological Tradition* states that 'the concept of social class, in distinction from the earlier concepts of hierarchy is late eighteenth century'. Asa Briggs also argues along similar lines (Briggs and Saville, 1967):

> The concept of social 'class' with all its attendant terminology
> was a product of the large-scale economic and social changes
> of the late eighteenth and early nineteenth centuries.... There
> was no dearth of social conflicts in pre-industrial society, but
> they were not conceived of at the time in straight class terms.
> The change in nomenclature in the late eighteenth and early
> nineteenth centuries reflected a basic change not only in men's
> ways of viewing society but in society itself.

Both Nisbet and Briggs ask *why* it was that social class developed at this time. Nisbet appears to be satisfied with a relatively simple answer: he accepts the view put forward by Ostrogorski that the move away from a 'continuous' system of ranking to a conflict situation of two opposed groups was due to the new kind of sub-ordination typical of industrialization. The personal contact be-tween worker and employer, characteristic of pre-industrial work situations, was replaced by an anonymous, 'abstract' relationship based exclusively on work and wages and the law of supply and demand. Workers ceased to be human dependents and became so many remote and often unseen factory hands.

Asa Briggs's very interesting essay shows how the use of the word 'class' developed during the early nineteenth century. His main point is that as consciousness of class developed and the concept crystallized, so the word 'class' was used more frequently and more precisely. Briggs attributes increased class-consciousness and power largely to a combination of the French and Industrial Revolutions (Briggs and Saville, 1967, pp. 62-3):

> The combined effect of the French and Industrial Revolutions, was to direct attention not to the powerlessness of the labourer but to the potential power of the 'working classes', whether hitched to the middle classes or, more ominously, relying on their own leaders.

Thompson's account of the *making* of the English working class is a much more detailed and complex analysis. His main point is that the class system did not simply develop by chance: it was the direct (if unintended) result of industrial and governmental policies. I will summarize this 'making' process under the following four headings:

(a) *destruction of traditional ways of life*—especially of what we would now call leisure pursuits;
(b) *changes in the work relationship*, especially for craftsmen, and the loss of meaning and dignity in work—*alienation*;
(c) *reduced standard of living*;
(d) *the growth of a conflict view of society*, partly due to (b) and (c) above, but also to deliberate political oppression, backed up by the economic ideology of *laissez-faire*.

(a) *Destruction of traditional ways of life* The story of the rapid increase in enclosures and the mechanization of agriculture is well known. The two processes broke up many rural communities and forced people into the growing towns. Even those who stayed in their villages had changes thrust upon them: not only were they deprived of common land, but game laws were tightened and penalties savagely enforced. Much of this repressive policy was justified by the view that the French Revolution had been caused by 'weakness' and that therefore peasants should be kept down; this political view was accompanied by the convenient economic argument that the price of labour should find its own level (see (d) below). In the towns, recreations were also deliberately restricted. There were two kinds of pressures and doctrines developing which tended to destroy traditional recreations and pastimes: the 'utilitarian' philosophy of the manufacturers, and the puritanical attitudes of the Methodists. Utilitarian philosophy, as interpreted by the manufacturers, stressed the value of work and discipline, and

34

condemned as levities any activities which were not 'useful' in the narrow sense of 'productive'. At the same time, Methodist tracts and sermons condemned 'profane' songs and dancing, together with anything in the arts or literature which was non-religious in character. Thus traditional forms of amusement began to disappear partly as a result of the decrease in leisure time available, and partly as a result of deliberate social and religious pressures: hours of work were very long, the old saints' days and holidays were almost completely abolished, and religious sanctions were invoked to enforce devotion to work rather than 'idle pleasures'.

Naturally, a whole way of life could not be entirely destroyed, and Thompson refers to 'underground' cultural activities which were handed on from ballad-singers and fairgrounds to the nineteenth-century music-hall and circus.

Richard Hoggart (1960, pp. 24-5) also refers to the survival, even up to the 1930s, of certain aspects of rural community life. But these were only a few remains—the way of life as a cultural whole had been effectively destroyed; much of what Bantock refers to as 'folk culture' disappeared completely. As far as this chapter is concerned, an important question is whether the folk culture of the country communities was eventually replaced by some kind of urban folk culture. This is outside the range of Thompson's research but it is an important question. According to some historians, a worthwhile alternative way of life did develop: Checkland (1964), for example, describes how music-halls developed from spontaneous displays of talent in taverns from the 1830s onwards. Music-halls spread from London to other big towns and eventually the songs were known throughout the country, so that some, like Thomas Hardy, feared that this would be a final blow to simple village culture. Checkland also shows how, later in the century, working men's clubs became important cultural centres: for debate, reading, games such as billiards and chess, as well as choral singing and brass bands in some parts of the country.

Clearly, important changes took place in working-class pastimes, and it is extremely difficult to come to any firm conclusion about the relative quality of the ways of life. Perhaps the greatest difference was in the separation of life into work and non-work categories which were much less meaningful before industrialization.

(b) *Changes in the work relationship* During this period (i.e. late eighteenth and early nineteenth centuries) there was a general tendency for agricultural labourers to become the rural poor, and for skilled craftsmen to become unskilled 'hands' in factories. In both cases work ceased to be a satisfactory and fulfilling activity:

for one group, work was denied; and for the other, work became a meaningless drudgery performed only to earn the wage at the end of the week: the 'cash nexus' became all-important. The idea of a *just or fair wage* was replaced by the dominant notion of *profit*, in farm and factory alike. Thompson (p. 248) quotes cases of farmers dismissing labourers even when work needed to be done, so that they would be paid something out of the poor rate rather than live entirely on wages. According to Thompson the system 'had a single tendency: to destroy the last vestige of control by the labourer over his own wage or working life'. In addition, as we have seen, the enclosure movement also destroyed the possibility of an agricultural labourer working for himself by grazing geese or pigs on the common. He became more and more dependent on an employer at the time when employers were less interested than ever before in their workers as human beings, and felt less responsibility for their welfare.

In the towns, skilled craftsmen and artisans such as carpenters frequently ceased to be independent and worked as hands in a 'strapping shop' under the supervision of a foreman; similarly, tailors who could not afford to buy their own cloth now became dependent on middlemen who set up 'sweat-shops'. London shoe-makers, Sheffield cutlers and many others found themselves degraded in much the same way. Agricultural labourers had lost their land, artisans lost their independence; both groups lost self-respect. Perhaps the most quoted example of loss of independence, status and eventually employment is the case of the hand-loom weavers. There has been much argument about the weavers, but most of the controversy is about the exact dates of the decline rather than the fact that these self-employed craftsmen either became workers in appalling conditions in factories or were deprived of work altogether. Few people now claim that life in a hand-loom weaver's cottage prior to industrialization was paradise, but it would be difficult not to see the growth of factories as a disaster for the majority of the weavers. Thompson indicates clearly (pp. 338-9), however, that what the weavers resisted was not simply working in a factory:

> the conflict was between two cultural modes or ways of life.... Even before the advent of power the woollen weavers disliked the hand-loom factories. They resented, first, the discipline; the factory bell or hooter; the time-keeping which over-rode ill-health, domestic arrangements, or the choice of more varied occupations.... Next they resented the effects upon family relationships of the factory system....

Changes in the work relation also had important effects on the family structure: in a weaver's family, women and children had certainly been expected to work, but the father of the family had always been the key figure in the unit; this was also changed by the factory system: 'skilled' work, such as it was, could be done by women and children; the men who were employed, now had to do the heavy lifting and carrying—they became intelligent beasts of burden rather than skilled workers. The whole nature of the relationship between man and work had been dramatically changed and this change represented a change in the whole way of life. Some historians and sociologists (e.g. Smelser, 1959) have suggested that the horrors have been exaggerated, but Thompson shows that although the extent of the physical suffering may well have been over-emphasized by some earlier historians (e.g. Hammond and Hammond, 1920), the dramatic changes in life-style must be undeniable. Thompson's main point is that this kind of change has to be related to class-consciousness and class-conflict. My own immediate interest is, of course, in *general cultural changes*, but they are clearly connected with the development of class-consciousness.

(c) *Reduced standard of living*   It is sometimes argued that although the early days of industrialization may have produced some hardship, workers were, on the whole, better off, at least in their standard of living. In the long run this may have been correct, but I want to concentrate on the *immediate* effects of industrialization, and with reference to the period under discussion two points have to be made. First, Thompson clearly shows how misleading it is to use *average* figures for wages and cost of living: even if average wages can be shown to be higher for certain years (and this is not beyond dispute), there was tremendous suffering for the thousands of workers below the average. Second, although a higher standard of living may eventually have been attained by the majority of the working-class, we must analyse carefully the long-term effects of those years of immediate hardship and deprivation. In other words, we have to ask what were the *lasting* effects of a fall in living standards accompanied by the other factors under consideration in this section?

But first of all we should look at the kind of hardship that was endured in these years. During the period of the French wars there was a tendency for both rents and food prices to rise. In 1795, for example, there were crop failures as well as difficulties of supply caused by the war, and prices rose dramatically. This was the year of 'Speenhamland'—the policy of regulating the subsidizing of wages out of rates according to the price of bread. (This had the demoralizing effect of men never earning enough wages to support their families even at minimum subsistence levels.) Food riots were common in the summer and autumn of that year, and there were several occasions when the Militia called out to disperse the riots took the part of the rioters.

This period of high food prices was also a time of increasing mechanization and unemployment. There was also a growing adherence by employers to the new economic doctrine that labour should be allowed to find its own natural price, according to the laws of supply and demand. At a time of increasing population and a declining demand for field labour this was bound to result in poverty and near starvation for the masses of agricultural workers —there was usually a large pool of reserve labour.

In towns the position was not much better. The organized structure of crafts and craft-apprenticeship was collapsing, traditional skills became obsolete and there was an abundance of cheap, unskilled labour available. In some towns Irish immigrants at first helped to swell the ranks of the unemployed looking for work. The process of wages finding their natural level certainly brought high profits to the employers, but lower standards of living for the workers. The result was, however, not simply a lowering of standards but in many cases social disintegration. The number of scroungers, beggars, paupers and petty criminals increased: 'Malnutrition was so distinct a feature of the textile towns that rickets were known on the continent as the English disease' (Checkland, p. 234).

After the war there was no immediate improvement: Cole and Postgate (1961, p. 239) quote Cobbett's *Rural Rides* to support their view that between 1815 and 1834 'labourers, employed and unemployed, were living ... under conditions of steadily increasing misery'. In most places the misery continued on into the 'hungry '40s'. Cole and Postgate assert (p. 304) that during these depressed years the distribution of the national income was changing in favour of the rich to such an extent that even those workers who were still in employment were living in abysmal poverty, and those thousands who were unemployed were destitute.

What long-lasting effects did such conditions of life have upon the culture, way of life and consciousness of working-class people? There is surprisingly little written on the subject. Such books as *The Common People* by Cole and Postgate usually stop short at descriptions of physical poverty, whereas what is also needed is some indication of general social life and cultural activities.

(d) *The growth of a conflict view of society* So far, I have concentrated mainly on the effects of the Industrial Revolution, but of major significance is the fact that class-consciousness was caused not only by increasing industrialization (with all the consequent problems described above) but by the combination of the Industrial Revolution and the fears, among the upper classes, which had been generated by the French Revolution. This combination of industrial changes—backed up by *laissez-faire* philosophy—and counter-revolutionary political doctrines resulted not only in exploitation but in oppression.

The French Revolution had stimulated enough radical political discussion in England to worry the upper classes and to provoke the government into such legislation as the famous 'Two Acts' (1795 and 1796) and the suspension of Habeas Corpus. The 'Two Acts' extended treason to speaking and writing and also controlled public meetings. The Acts may be seen as 'normal' wartime measures or as part of a whole process of panic and repressive legislation (Thompson, p. 64):

> There have always persisted popular attitudes to crime, amounting at times to an unwritten code, quite distinct from the laws of the land. Certain crimes were outlawed by both codes: a wife or child murderer would be pelted and execrated on the way to Tyburn.... But other crimes were actively condoned by whole communities—coining, poaching, the evasion of taxes ... or excise or the press-gang. Smuggling communities lived in a state of constant war with authorities....
>
> This distinction between the legal code and the unwritten popular code is a commonplace at any time. But rarely have the two codes been more sharply distinguished from each other than in the second half of the eighteenth century ... in the years between the Restoration (1660) and the death of George III (1820) the number of capital offences was increased by about 190 ... 63 of those were added in the years 1760-1810. Not only petty theft, but primitive forms of industrial rebellion —destroying a silk loom, throwing down fences when commons were closed, and firing corn ricks—were to be punished by death.... The commercial expansion, the enclosure movement, the early years of the Industrial Revolution—all took place within the shadows of the gallows.

This passage sums up the changing atmosphere in England up to the Reform Bill 1832. One way of life had broken down, and any action by those who had suffered was interpreted as revolutionary by the ruling class and eventually resulted in more repression and hostility.

To these specific examples mentioned by Thompson might be added the well-known Combination Acts (1799-1800) which out-lawed any possibility of workers improving their pay and conditions by Trade Union activities. It is interesting to note that it was not simply a question of oppression by means of legislation, but of the enforcement of legislation. For example, in theory the Acts not only prevented collective bargaining by workers but also combinations of employers; but in practice official action was never taken against employers, despite a number of attempts by radicals to enforce this aspect of the law (Cole and Postgate, 1961, p. 177):

> the story of the years from 1800-1815 is industrially one of
> defeat and oppression. The Acts placed the working men at
> the mercy of two classes, the English gentlemen and the
> English employers. They depended on the fairness of the first
> for the application of the law (as magistrates), and on either
> for the law to be put in motion—for the magistrates, using spies
> and informers, were often more active than the employers in
> starting prosecutions.

Deprived of the traditional, customary rules applying to servant and master, and prevented by the new legal machinery from resorting to Trade Union or other kinds of collective activity, the workers turned to rioting and violence. Luddism was but one of the by-products of political and economic oppression.

What effect did this oppression have on the attitudes and consciousness of working people? Thompson clearly believes (p. 217) that the destruction of a traditional way of life, changes in the work relationship, a reduced standard of living, and above all, the political and economic oppression forced the working-class into what he describes as 'political and social apartheid':

> We can now see something of the truly catastrophic nature
> of the Industrial Revolution; as well as some of the reasons
> why the English working-class took form in those years. The
> people were subjected simultaneously to an intensification of
> two intolerable forms of relationship: those of economic
> exploitation and of political oppression. Relations between
> employer and labourer were becoming both harsher and less
> personal; and while it is true that this increased the potential
> freedom of the worker, since the hired farm servant or the
> journeyman in domestic industry was (in Toynbee's words)
> 'halted half-way between the position of the serf and the
> position of the citizen', this 'freedom' meant that he felt his
> unfreedom more. But at each point where he sought to resist
> exploitation, he was met by the forces of employer or State,
> and commonly of both.

Long-term Results Another important question is also relevant at this stage. Was the change in culture, of which class-consciousness formed part, merely a change in direction or did it result in a culture which was inferior or 'damaged' in some ways? Writers as different politically as Bantock on the one hand and Cole and Postgate on the other, seem to assume that working-class culture was 'damaged' in some respects by the transition. Bantock, for example, talks of the loss of folk culture and the fact that it has not been effectively replaced; Cole and Postgate go even further when they talk of the working-class being psychologically 'diseased'. They justify their use of this term by the supposedly irrational aspects of working-class life—such as turning to prophetic and Messianic religions, and their behaviour at public meetings, such as Chartist gatherings, which amounted to mass hysteria. To account for their 'irrational' behaviour, Cole and Postgate suggest that living conditions were so bad that 'escapist' solutions were adopted on a wide scale.

Checkland also refers to the 'grave social damage' caused by the breakdown of family ties and customs, and the hordes of homeless children in the great cities.

Cole and Postgate also give the impression (p. 586) that certain aspects of this early nineteenth century suffering lasted at least until the end of the nineteenth century (and probably later):

When Robert Lowe, as Chancellor of the Exchequer, proposed a tax upon matches which could have thrown a number of East End women out of work, Westminster was invaded by a 'deputation' of filthy and haggard harridans whom the London which saw them for the first time considered to be only half human. When Burns spoke upon Tower Hill to his dockers only a small part of his speeches was devoted to Union demands: a large section was turned to urging them to behave as human beings—not to beat their wives, not to fight one another savagely, not to drink themselves stupid at the first opportunity.

The culture of poverty

Other writers have examined the lives of groups of people living under social conditions similar to those described above, and have attempted to make generalizations about 'the culture of poverty'. Maria Ossowska, for example, has written about the kinds of culture of poverty in Mexico City described by Oscar Lewis. She suggests that a poverty sub-culture is characterized by lack of privacy, gregariousness, alcoholism, physical violence, a more permissive attitude to sex, family solidarity and a generally fatalistic attitude towards life accompanied by a distrust of authority.

A number of points have to be examined: first the extent to

which Bantock, Cole and Postgate and others are correct in diagnosing not merely cultural change but working-class cultural inferiority in the nineteenth century; secondly, even if there were temporary 'damage' in the nineteenth century, has this been rectified in the twentieth century? Some of the features of the culture of poverty have sometimes been attributed to twentieth-century, working-class life-styles, but this may well be due to lack of clear distinction between the twentieth-century working-class and the twentieth-century poor or severely disadvantaged.

But other difficulties also arise in this kind of analysis. For example, if we accept Cole and Postgate's argument about the decline in working-class life in the nineteenth century, we should also look carefully at middle-class standards. Cole and Postgate seem to indicate (p. 308) a general decline in cultural standards in the nineteenth century :

> Not unnaturally, in such a regime the arts which made life pleasant declined and disappeared. Painting and music touched a new low level of vulgarity; architecture destroyed city after city and covered the face of Britain with bestial ugliness which probably can never be wholly undone. Only literature survived.

Cole and Postgate might have added a few more undesirable cultural characteristics acquired by the middle-classes during the nineteenth century : such as avarice, ruthlessness, selfish individualism, etc.

Perhaps the analogy of health and disease applied to culture by Cole and Postgate is more misleading than helpful. It would be more in keeping with general anthropological thinking to avoid such blanket descriptions or value-judgments and talk, instead, of specific strengths and weaknesses of particular cultures for particular purposes. All cultures, seen from outside, appear to possess certain advantages in coping with some aspects of life and certain disadvantages in other respects. The culture of poverty described by Ossowska may be seen as a 'realistic' adjustment to a very harsh environment in which personal effort might not make much difference. Similarly the working-class adjustment to the hostile urban environment in the eighteenth and nineteenth centuries may have been effective in as much as it facilitated survival. But we also have to ask whether, in the long run, certain communities have found themselves in cultural dead-ends, i.e. living in a way which limits opportunities outside the sub-culture. If we now want to abolish poverty must we destroy the culture of poverty? I would suggest that it is difficult to see how a culture can survive without its social and economic environment, therefore the culture of poverty should eventually disappear; but it should be stressed that this is *not* the same as working-class culture.

Class and cultural differences

Given that extremely important social class differences emerged during the nineteenth century it is still misleading to see cultural pluralism or fragmentation of culture on purely social-class lines. Notwithstanding the evidence presented by Thompson and others, it is particularly dangerous to associate 'high culture' exclusively with upper and middle-classes. Some of those who criticize schools for passing on middle-class culture to working-class children are guilty of an enormous over-simplification in this respect. In what sense is an appreciation of literature more middle-class than working-class? And to stray further from high culture into general culture, but into an area where the same class argument has been applied, in what sense are mathematics, science and history middle-class?

I would not wish to underestimate the importance of social class and cultural differences, but it is all too easy to move from statistical probability based on slight differences in percentages to vast but invalid generalizations. For example, it is true that the average height of middle-class men and women is greater than the average height of working-class men and women: it is not true that all middle-class people are tall and all the working-class are short. This is an obvious physical example, but equally absurd cultural generalizations sometimes get taken seriously: for example, that middle-class adults read and working-class adults do not. Hard data on this subject are difficult to come by, but such evidence as we have (Roberts, 1970, p. 15) is certainly of interest in this respect, and often does not support 'common sense' prejudices or pre-suppositions:

> Apart from leisure time being distributed fairly evenly throughout society, and apart from this leisure time occurring in a common rhythm throughout the population, the activities with which people fill their leisure display certain basic ingredients throughout the community. This is another sense in which as far as leisure is concerned, Britain can now be described as an egalitarian society. There are no sharp cleavages distinguishing the leisure of one stratum of society from another. In spite of the differences in incomes and financial resources that exist, the leisure pursuits adopted throughout society are similar to a remarkable degree.

The evidence on which Roberts, and others, base this view consists of BBC and ITV audience and viewing research and other kinds of surveys of interests and pastimes. Typically, such surveys show that apart from a few activities such as watching television, which has a very wide appeal, most leisure pursuits appeal to only a small minority of the population, even when the sample is broken down into class and age groups. In other words, it is true to say that, for example, more middle-class people go to the opera than working-class, but since this is only a tiny minority, it is nonsense to talk of opera as middle-class.

Probably the most comprehensive recent survey of leisure pursuits is *Planning for Leisure* (Sillitoe, 1969). Once again, there was surprisingly little difference shown between occupational groups. One of the biggest differences was on 'popularity' of gardening as a leisure pursuit (it is more middle-class than working-class!), but as Sillitoe points out (p. 51): 'The most probable reason for the socio-economic difference in gardening is that the top groups are more likely to have a garden.'

Similarly the relation between class and certain kinds of outdoor activities was less important than the possession of a car.

All surveys are agreed that one of the major forms of leisure pastimes is watching television—for all classes. Once again it is true to say that there is a tendency for more middle-class people to watch BBC rather than ITV (and vice versa) but it would be non-sense to talk of 'middle-class BBC' and 'working-class ITV'. In a study of plays on both BBC and ITV, for example, the following points were made by McQuail (1970): apart from a general tendency for BBC play audiences to include more middle-class respondents, social class was not a significant factor either in decisions about what to watch or in the response to the play. Occupational differences were almost totally unrelated to reactions to any of the plays; education was slightly more important than class but was still only marginal. Age and sex differences were more important than occupation or education.

Similar findings have been repeated by other researchers (here and in the USA). For example, M. Abrams (1959) found no differences in media habits between the upper 1 per cent and the rest of the population; the Granada Survey in 1959 found only very slight differences in the social class composition of various audiences (McQuail, 1970, p. 348):

On the basis of a sample of over 15,000 adults, Abrams reported in 1959 that almost no differences in media habits could be distinguished between the upper 1% and the remainder. The Granada Viewership Survey, relating to the same year, also showed only very slight differences in the social class composition of the audiences for different categories of television programme.

Another aspect of the myth of middle-class culture, to which reference has already been made, is that middle-class people read and working-class people do not. This is once again very far from the truth. Despite methodological difficulties in defining both 'reading' and 'books' it is clear that middle-class, better-educated adults tend to be more 'bookish', but by no means all middle-class adults are 'readers'—they, like working-class adults, are much more likely to spend their time watching television. Even newspaper reading is much less class-linked than is often popularly supposed: for example (Tunstall, 1970), less than half of *Observer* readers are in the AB category (i.e. professional, managerial and better-paid white collar workers).

Class and reading

Thus despite important differences between classes in traditions and consciousness, there does seem to exist a common culture in a very meaningful sense. Even Bantock's claim that we should seek a different kind of curriculum for the majority of working-class pupils *because their tradition is a non-literary one* does not stand up to close inspection of the historical facts. First, if we look back beyond the nineteenth century it is by no means clear that there was a very sharp division between the classes in their reading habits: Altick (1957) clearly showed a long working-class tradition of reading and appreciation of being read to. Second, in so far as it is true that reading did decline among the working-class in the nineteenth century, this can be seen to be very largely the result of different patterns of work and leisure brought about by the growth of industrialization and urbanization, i.e. many working-class people had neither sufficient leisure time nor accommodation for reading. On the other hand, we know little about differences in desire to read. Thirdly, there is certainly some evidence during the nineteenth century of some working-class distaste for reading, but it is often attributable to working-class people resenting being 'got at' by their supposed social superiors—sometimes in the form of meddlesome middle-class women who persuaded slum-dwellers to hand over a penny a week until the price of a bible had been accumulated, sometimes amateur missionaries selling various kinds of 'wholesome' tracts designed to improve the masses (Altick, pp. 107-8):

The tract bearers' motives were too obvious to be mistaken.

45

Beneath the veneer of altruism could be seen all too plainly the image of class interest. Tracts were supposed to keep one from thinking wicked Chartist thoughts, to make one content with his empty stomach and stench-filled hovel.

The utilitarian do-gooders probably produced results little less harmful (op. cit., p. 132):

Profoundly aware that each passing moment was precious and that life had to be lived with the utmost methodicalness, they deplored what they called the habit of 'desultory reading'. If one were to read at all, it should be with a fixed end in mind, not a random flitting from one subject to another. This was implicit in the whole gospel of self-improvement that sprang from the union of evangelicism and Benthamism. The ambitious artisan was to share in the diffusion of useful knowledge, not by following his own inclinations but by systematically reading what he had to learn in order to become a better workman. Reading for the mere sake of reading—finding amusement in one book, instruction in a second, a bit of inspiration in a third—could not be too severely condemned.

This feeling that reading was at least idle and wasteful and at worst dangerous in the hands of the masses persisted throughout the nineteenth century, and Altick (p. 140) describes in great detail 'how the governing middle-class sought to withhold from the newly literate multitude the sort of reading that Herschel and Dickens insisted they needed above all—reading that would give them simple pleasure after a hard day's work.'

This withholding attitude was, of course, also associated with the prevailing middle-class feelings about elementary education. Moreover, the way that reading was taught in elementary schools must often have been enough to produce a lasting distaste for the printed word.

But despite all these handicaps the evidence for a considerable working-class readership in the nineteenth century is overwhelming. Altick quotes a number of sources to support his view that cheaper printing resulted in a good deal of reading and book-buying by the working-class as well as by middle-class readers.

Altick is not alone in this view: such research as *Fiction for the Working Man 1830-50* by L. James (1963), and *The British Working Class Reader 1790-1848* by R. K. Webb (1955), also demonstrate that reading in the nineteenth century was by no means confined to the upper and middle classes. Similar views can also sometimes be found in general historical accounts of the nineteenth century (Checkland, p. 270):

There was also a serious reading element among the workers, for the excitement of the new world opened by the printed page could be infectious. Durham miners went to school with their own children to learn to read; the Working Men's College in St. Pancras founded in 1854 by F. D. Maurice succeeded because it was based upon the belief that adult education must be reciprocal between teachers and taught. Efforts were made, especially by the Society for the Diffusion of Useful Knowledge, founded in 1827, the Working Men's Union, started in 1852, and the Pure Literature Society, established in 1855, to make good books available.

Today the evidence that exists seems to relate reading with housing conditions and levels of formal education rather than with class *per se* (Mann, 1971; Benge, 1970). A number of studies of the use of public libraries, for example, shows that although there are class differences in membership and reading habits, they are less marked than is often expected. Just as some teachers are beginning to question their own attitudes rather than assume that something is wrong with the pupils, so librarians are beginning to question the middle-class, dismal and rejecting image that libraries are felt to possess (see Groombridge, 1970; Luckham, 1971; Stevens, 1972). There is nothing in the literature on reading to support the view that the working-class should be regarded either as non-literary or as completely different from middle-class people in their reading habits.

Class-consciousness: common culture

There is another more general reason for doubting the validity of suggesting different kinds of curriculum for working-class and middle-class children. Thompson argues his case very convincingly and, in my view, establishes his thesis that by the 1830s class-consciousness had been developed in the working-class—the working-class had been 'made' by that time. This is very important for my analysis and so are the details provided by Thompson concerning the changes in working-class life and the establishment of some kinds of working-class sub-cultures. But Thompson's account virtually stops in 1832 and it is essential to try to take the story on from there. Moorhouse (1973), for example, argues that by the second half of the nineteenth century the ruling class had learned their lesson and set out to win over not only the lower middle-class but the workers themselves. This was achieved, according to Moorhouse, by appearing to share political power but in reality retaining it. To what extent this attempt to move away

47

from a conflict situation has been successful is certainly open to debate, but the existence today of very large numbers of working-class Conservatives is a factor which cannot be easily dismissed. Even if real power has been preserved in the hands of the few, it is probable that we have moved away from the nineteenth-century 'Two Nations'/two cultures kind of society, and that the picture is now much more complicated and blurred. It looks as though working-class consciousness grew up during the eighteenth and early nineteenth centuries, but has been modified to some extent during the late nineteenth and the twentieth centuries.

Michael Mann (1973) has reviewed the whole question of contemporary class-consciousness in a most useful way. Mann does not accept the 'end of ideology' thesis by which it is supposed that part of the 'logic of industrialization' is the institutionalization of conflict into co-operation plus wage-bargaining (i.e. that the opposing interests of management and workers are recognized as such, but are harnessed into negotiating machinery designed to keep the system going); nor does he accept the Marxist view of inevitable class conflict and revolution. Mann suggests that class-consciousness is a complex phenomenon which needs to be subdivided into class *identity*, class *opposition*, class *totality* (i.e. class as the defining characteristic of the whole society), and finally the conception of an *alternative society*. Mann suggests that the existence of the first two does not necessarily imply the existence of the other two (full consciousness up to a revolutionary level). The obstacle to this kind of class-consciousness is the hegemonic nature of capitalist society, i.e. the fact that workers' lives are segmented or broken down into separate compartments—work, consumption, politics etc. It seems fairly well established that in their work situation many (but not all) working-class men are 'alienated' and feel both a class identity and opposition. But this does not necessarily flow over into non-work situations. Argyris (1964) is quoted to show that workers tend to develop psychological defence mechanisms against objective reality, such as rationalization, projection, day-dreaming, apathy and fatalism, but it is not clear to what extent these become part of the non-work personality; if they did develop such symptoms it would be evidence for the kind of psychological 'damage' discussed earlier in the chapter in relation to eighteenth- and nineteenth-century working conditions. According to Kornhauser (1965), men who stay in boring, routine, 'depriving' jobs for many years do develop fatalistic views about life in general. Part of this fatalism is an acceptance of an inferior position in the hierarchy, which would perhaps flow over into an attitude of 'not for the likes of us' for some general cultural activities such as theatre. But Mann stresses that the picture which emerges from such studies is a very complex one—for example, 'the most alienated workers are not the most revolutionary, for the necessary confidence in their own power is lacking' (Mann, p. 91).

Class and educational policy

Stemming from such analyses, I want to suggest four important implications for education: first, although I would accept Thompson's thesis that working-class consciousness was firmly established by 1832, I would also suggest that important changes may have taken place since 1832 regarding working-class consciousness and culture; second, there is some support for the view that some working-class sub-cultures are psychologically 'unhealthy', disadvantaged or impoverished as a result of appalling working and living conditions; but this should not lead us into the trap of making generalizations about all working-class sub-cultures; and finally, this should make us very cautious about accepting the idea of constructing a curriculum to suit the sub-culture—we may want to begin with the immediate working-class environment but we should also certainly look beyond it. Moreover, whatever may have been the social origins of such 'high' culture activities as music, literature, art and drama, it is certainly very difficult to identify high culture with middle-class culture today.

Thus it is difficult *now* to see any validity in either right-wing or left-wing objections to schools attempting to transmit a common culture by means of deliberate curriculum planning. It may be true, of course, that in some ways many schools could be said to be middle-class institutions if the teachers are middle-class in background or have been effectively socialized by middle-class teachers throughout their own education. But to accept that most teachers are middle-class is very different from accepting that *everything* that the school offers is middle-class culture and, therefore, of no value to working-class children. I would accept Jackson and Marsden's (1962) view that some schools are misguided in their emphasis on middle-class manners, etiquette and low level middle-class values, but this is quite different from saying that the *knowledge* that grammar schools in the past have tried to transmit is middle-class. The point of view I am expressing is quite different from this: it is true that schools have in the past tended to emphasize middle-class etiquette and have not given enough attention to the transmission of (classless) knowledge and high-level moral principles; i.e. there is evidence to show that many teachers are more upset by 'bad' behaviour of pupils than by their failure to acquire knowledge. Many schools devote more time and energy to fussing about uniform, length of hair, etc., than to greed and selfishness.

The fact that teachers themselves appear to confound questions of etiquette, moral behaviour and academic standards is itself important. Many schools also over-emphasize the extrinsic motives for acquiring knowledge (passing examinations and getting 'good' jobs), but this is quite different from saying that the knowledge itself is of no value. What has to be argued out is what kind of knowledge, values and experience are worthwhile for all pupils, and then how can schools transmit this selection from the culture to *all* pupils in a way which is not insulting or rejecting. This is partly a problem of teacher training: teachers must not only know what to teach but also how to communicate with children whose background is different from their own.

I have deliberately avoided trying to describe the positive aspects of contemporary working-class life. It does seem to me that many qualities exist such as co-operativeness and warmth of personal relationships, but these are not the raw material of curriculum planning. This does not imply that such qualities are unimportant or that schools could not do more to foster them rather than the usual competitiveness and individual achievement, but it is difficult to see them as centrally important in curriculum planning, although they might be important features of moral education which has been sadly neglected (see Chapter 6).

There is another problem connected with planning a common curriculum that has not yet been dealt with. The problem is that even if the content and organization of the curriculum *provided* for the pupils is common, does it follow that the pupils will *receive* this content as common? It is possible that children from different backgrounds and of different levels of ability will receive a common curriculum in a highly differentiated way. To a certain extent this is a question of depth and breadth which White has discussed (1973, pp. 61-72): One of the aims of a common curriculum is to establish a basic minimum of compulsory content which can be effectively evaluated and also added to in terms of depth of understanding. In this sense no two pupils will receive exactly the same from the curriculum, but they should all share an understanding of the basic minimum. One of the features of a common curriculum (to be discussed in Chapter 6) is precisely how to organize experience and worthwhile knowledge in a way which will make a basic, common understanding possible. It may also be objected that even this common, basic minimum may be received differently by children from different sub-cultures: part of the purpose of this chapter was to argue that, in some ways, social class/sub-cultural differences may have been exaggerated. The question will be examined again in Chapter 4.

Summary

In this chapter, I have attempted:
1. To show how class-consciousness and separate class structures developed during the eighteenth and nineteenth centuries;
2. to examine the suggestion that the working-class culture that developed was inferior or even diseased;
3. to suggest that the view that the 'healthy/diseased' analogy was misleading, and that it would be more appropriate to see cultures (and sub-cultures) in terms of relative strengths and weaknesses for specific purposes;
4. to introduce the idea that during the nineteenth century, 'middle-class culture' also suffered from the aftermath of the Industrial Revolution, and writers such as Cole and Postgate have complained of low standards, especially in the visual arts; some would also argue that middle-class people today tend to be more greedy, selfish and ruthless than members of the working-class;
5. to argue that in terms of 'high culture' it is very misleading to see art, music and literature as middle-class, and that it is even more ridiculous to see science, mathematics and history as middle-class;
6. finally, to suggest that whilst it may be true that some schools spend a good deal of time trying to pass on trivial aspects of lower middle-class manners and etiquette, it does not necessarily follow that everything that such schools try to transmit is trivial or class-based. The main content of the curriculum—knowledge —should be classless, and so could the means of transmission or teaching-style, but this will require major changes in teacher behaviour. The problem of transmitting a selection from common culture is not only a question of knowledge; it also involves difficult questions of teacher-pupil relationships.

4

Sociology, knowledge and the curriculum

In Chapter 3 I argued that there were no convincing arguments against the existence of some elements of a common culture in our society—sufficient at least as a basis for a common curriculum, which is not to deny the importance of sub-cultural differences. The educational problem, therefore, is a combination of curriculum planning and changing some teachers' attitudes and behaviour towards their pupils (even a 'perfect' curriculum will not work without teachers who respect and understand their pupils). Before analysing the problem of making a selection from the culture—planning a curriculum—it will be necessary to examine the whole question of knowledge and curriculum from the perspective of the sociology of knowledge. So far, I have touched on this aspect of knowledge without any detailed examination of it.

Marx

It has sometimes been suggested that much of modern sociology is a debate with the ghost of Marx. To some extent this is true of a great deal of the current controversy about knowledge and education. Marx's view of knowledge and class may be summarized as follows: the dominant view of knowledge in society is the view of the ruling class. In feudal times the dominant view of knowledge was the view of the ruling nobility. In modern capitalist society the prevailing view of knowledge is a bourgeois one. Art, literature, music, morality, history and philosophy are 'bourgeois representations'. Ultimately, according to Marx, this bourgeois view of reality will be overthrown by the proletarian 'culture' and world view. Meanwhile, he suggests that the only way of avoiding seeing the world through bourgeois eyes is to develop a disciplined awareness of the need for revolution and an identification with the interests of the working-class. Much of the later discussion of knowledge, culture and education is based on this Marxian view, or on variations and contradictions of it.

Mannheim

Karl Mannheim's view of the relation between class, ideology and knowledge is on the same lines as Marx but with a different—non-revolutionary—interpretation. Mannheim was greatly concerned with the fact that different sections of the community—different social classes—have only *limited* ways of perceiving reality or have only limited access to knowledge. In this respect his views were very similar to those of Marx. Unlike Marx, Mannheim did not make qualitative judgments about the differences between the social levels. He did not think that the bourgeois view of reality was 'wrong' or superior or inferior to the proletarian view, but merely that each class possessed *limited* views of reality because of their different backgrounds and social perspectives. Essentially the two groups perceived the world differently because they had been socialized differently, and had acquired different sets of skills and, above all, different kinds of knowledge. Like Marx, however, Mannheim argued that society determines not only the appearance but also the content of 'ideation' (i.e. subject matter as well as subjects), except in the case of mathematics and some kinds of science. Mannheim used the word 'ideology' in a very special, narrow sense. By ideology Mannheim meant the false, or limited, view of reality held by the ruling class. This view of reality was necessarily distorted, partly because it was incomplete, and partly because it was a conservative or reactionary view of reality, the ruling class having a vested interest in preserving the existing order of things. Once again there are similarities here with the Marxist argument. Mannheim, like Marx, thought that it was possible for individuals to see the world in a less limited way. The way to achieve this 'enlightenment' was to learn to see reality from as many of the different social positions as possible. Mannheim thought that the group which was most likely to develop this kind of classless perception was the 'socially unattached intelligentsia'. This group, according to Mannheim, was relatively free of class interests, containing many members who were marginal in the sense that they had moved out of one class without becoming fully committed to the reality system of their new class. This judgment was, of course, based on speculation rather than evidence.

One of the things Marx and Mannheim had in common was that they both realized that the process by which human beings perceive reality is much more complicated than a camera taking a photograph of physical objects. Human beings observing reality employ a system of interpretations derived from their 'culture'; cultures differ to some extent; therefore members of different cultures see the world differently; members of the same culture, but at different levels within it, also see the world differently. Another point of similarity between Marx and Mannheim is their stress on class, and the importance of the ruling class in the distribution of knowledge and the stratification of knowledge (i.e. *who* possesses knowledge, and *what* kind of knowledge is valued). They also agreed that certain kinds of knowledge were less likely to be 'distorted' than others—they both thought of science and mathematics as comparatively free of ideological or class distortion.

One of the difficulties with both Marx and Mannheim is that their argument that ideas are a product of social position can be applied to all their own writings. For example, Bertrand Russell (1946, p. 751) made the following remark in his discussion of Marx, but it could equally well be turned against Mannheim:

> No man would engage in the pursuit of philosophy if he thought that *all* philosophy is *merely* an expression of irrational bias. But every philosopher will agree that many other philosophers have been actuated by bias, and have had extra-rational reasons, of which they were usually unconscious, for many of their opinions. Marx, like the rest, believes in the truth of his own doctrines; he does not regard them as nothing but an expression of the feelings natural to a rebellious middle-class German Jew in the middle of the nineteenth century.

We have to ask why should Marx, Mannheim and others who write in this deterministic way, be exempted from their own doctrines? If what they say is also merely the result of class bias or social position, why should we pay any attention to them? Mannheim's attempt to escape from the logic of the position by creating a bias-free group called the 'socially unattached intelligentsia' is not convincing. Popper (1966) dismisses all such attempts to justify 'individual enlightenment' and proposes instead that the only way to ensure freedom from bias is to submit one's ideas to the scientific scrutiny of an academic community where open criticism prevails and ensures rationality. Russell's comments on Marx would be resolved in the same way—the fact that Marx was a nineteenth-century German middle-class Jew is irrelevant to a judgment about whether he was right or wrong on specific issues; such a judgment can only be arrived at by means of the public, objective criteria of a philosophical, economic or sociological community. If disagreement exists within the academic community, this may be due to the ambiguity of the writer or to lack of total agreement within the community. This position is not without difficulties, but to try to relate *all* views to social bias is clearly, logically untenable.

Berger and Luckman

A more recent work on the same theme, which has been widely read, is Peter Berger and Thomas Luckman's *The Social Construction of Reality*. In this book Berger and Luckman appear to go further than Mannheim and suggest that *all* knowledge is socially constructed, that is, interpreted or filtered through the culture of those acquiring the knowledge. This view is in one sense a truism, since knowledge must indeed be social—i.e. shared by people—if it is to be knowledge at all. What Berger and Luckman appear to mean is that reality is interpreted differently by different social groups. It is not clear to what extent Berger and Luckman agree with Marx and Mannheim about mathematics and science being interpretation-free or class-free. The major difference between Berger and Luckman and Mannheim, however, is that for the authors of *Social Construction of Reality* knowledge *as a whole* is regarded as being socially constructed—that is, involves 'common sense reality' as well as academic subjects such as history, economics and political science. Their major contribution is that they suggest that sociology of knowledge must begin with the common-sense view of reality rather than with the history of ideas or the study of academic forms of knowledge. They criticize earlier writers on the sociology of knowledge, such as Mannheim, for ignoring the major area of 'common sense, everyday knowledge'.

All of this is relevant to the arguments I have outlined in Chapter 3. If different sections of the community, different social classes, do possess different views of reality, then this would make a common curriculum much more difficult to plan (but not necessarily impossible). So one important question will be, *to what extent* are these views of reality different? Another problem would be to decide between Marx and Mannheim—that is, to decide whether proletarian culture really is superior to bourgeois culture, or whether we accept Mannheim's idea of educating people into the kind of knowledge possessed by the socially unattached intelligentsia, i.e. academic knowledge.

It is very difficult to glean from Marx's writings the specific ways in which proletarian culture is to be regarded as superior. Other writers have mentioned such qualities as warmth of personal relations, co-operativeness, etc., but Marx seemed to be more concerned with the working-class closeness to 'real' work and therefore to the immediate mastery of the environment. It may be that

Marx simply relied on his prediction of the inevitability of the bourgeois culture being superseded by the proletarian (i.e. it was 'superior' because it would win in the end). It is precisely this kind of 'historicist' argument relying on inevitability, that has attracted the criticism of Popper (1966) and others. On the other hand, Mannheim's view that a non-ideological perception of reality could be made possible by studying the various interpretations of different social strata has an appeal for educationists, although there are problems involved in identifying the specific areas for study. Berger and Luckman do not attempt to relate their view of sociology of knowledge to educational problems, but there *are* important links; for example, their views might reinforce the opinion of those educationists who urge that teaching should begin from the pupils' common-sense reality and work outwards from there to the non-common-sense reality of academic subjects or disciplines, rather than in the tradition of the 'grammar school' teaching which has tended to focus on the academic subject and ignore or reject everyday reality. (See Barnes, *et al.*, 1969.)

Young

Until recently, very little has been written on applying the sociology of knowledge to educational problems—apart from the early work by Mannheim. But in 1971 M. F. D. Young edited a book which has given rise to a great deal of discussion in educational circles. Young's approach to this question not only directs some fundamental questions derived from the sociology of knowledge to educational problems, but also involves a radical critique of previous work in the sociology of education. It is, therefore, difficult to do justice to Young and his colleagues without saying something, however briefly and inadequately, about the sociology of education as a field of study.

It has often been argued that sociology as a subject, emerged in Western Europe as a response to the problems of rapid social change—the disorder, or even social disintegration, which were seen to be the results of the Industrial Revolution and the French Revolution. Much of Durkheim's writing, for example, was concerned with the possibility of the breakdown of social life following the loss of customary norms and values which had in the past been provided by the Church or the personal bonds of a society based on mechanical solidarity. Thus, although sociologists are often regarded as 'left-wing', it is ironic that classical sociology has been largely conservative in its outlook, concerned with social order, social control and consensus. The dominant influence of sociology, especially in the USA, has been a 'functionalist' school which stresses consensus rather than conflict, stability rather than change; accordingly, education has often been seen as a socializing agency, passing on traditional norms and values, and preparing the young to 'fit in' to their society.

I have deliberately simplified, and perhaps distorted, the development of sociology and the position within it of the sociology of education, in order to highlight the aspects that Young and others have criticized. Essentially, they criticize sociologists for 'taking' problems rather than 'making' them. For example, in the sociology of education the 'problem' of working-class pupils' under-achievement has been 'taken' or accepted by sociologists, when what they ought to be doing, according to Young, is questioning the nature of the achievement which is demanded by schools at present. One of the problems that Young suggests should have been 'made' is the nature of educational knowledge. 'What counts as knowledge' in schools should be submitted to careful sociological analysis rather than 'taken for granted'.

This new direction on the sociology of education is clearly connected with a new trend in general sociology—the view that 'common-sense' or 'taken for granted' views have to be questioned; the view that sociology itself rests on certain kinds of ideological pre-suppositions, and if we are to understand the social world we must get beyond these pre-suppositions, however well-established and institutionalized they may be.

Normative and interpretive paradigms

This dissatisfaction with mainstream sociology of education seems to be inspired by a number of different kinds of thinking. The first, a desire to apply the sociology of knowledge to the curriculum, has already been mentioned; the second is a radical, post-Marxian, view of society which looks critically at established institutions and is sympathetic to the view that schools are helping to preserve a corrupt and unjust society; the third is a phenomenological view of reality which questions the validity of common-sense or well-established ways of examining society (see p. 64 for a description of phenomenology). All of these are grouped together and referred to by Young as the *interpretive paradigm*, as opposed to the conventional *'normative'* paradigm in sociology. But to describe this grouping of views as the interpretive paradigm is somewhat misleading : one of the difficulties of interpreting what is meant by some of those new directions for the sociology of education is that the different strands behind the thinking get twisted occasionally, and also that there is a tendency to switch from one level of argument to another. It is, however, very important to distinguish between the different kinds of argument being employed, some of which are much more credible than others. It is especially necessary to apply to some aspects of Young's argument some of the work done by philosophers on the nature of knowledge. (See also Wilson, T. P., 1971, for another view of the normative and interpretive paradigms.)

I shall not attempt to summarize the whole book but will instead abstract five different levels of what seems to me to be the approach central to Young's *Knowledge and Control* (1971). The five levels I wish to examine are as follows:

Level 1 That the present structure and organization of education in our society serves to preserve the *status quo* in an unjust society—this level is particularly concerned with questions such as the *social distribution of knowledge*.

Level 2 That in particular the *content* of education—the selection of knowledge for transmission by schools—should be *made* into a problem for critical examination rather than be taken for granted; this level is concerned with *what counts for knowledge in our society, and the stratification of knowledge*.

Level 3 That *subject barriers are arbitrary and artificial*, existing largely for the convenience of those in control of education.

Level 4 That *all knowledge is socially constructed*.

Level 5 That not only knowledge but *rationality itself is merely a convention*.

Central to Young's argument is also the notion that the pupil should not be 'taken' as the problem but that teachers and schools should be 'made' into the problem. This aspect of the 'interpretive paradigm' seems to me to be an extremely valuable, but non-controversial, contribution to the sociology of education. For reasons of brevity, I refer to the above views collectively as Young's: I well appreciate that not all five levels would be shared by all the contributors to *Knowledge and Control*, as Young makes clear in his introduction (pp. 2-3). In particular I would agree with Pring (1972) that Bernstein's contribution to the book does not make exaggerated claims for the sociology of knowledge: in my terms Bernstein's essay is largely confined to Levels 1 and 2 above. Bernstein seems to have been much more aware than Young and Esland of Gurvitch's warning (1971, pp. 10-11) about the need to avoid the danger of making the sociology of knowledge attempt too much:

the sociologist of knowledge must never pose the problem

of validity and value of signs, symbols, concepts, ideas and judgments that he meets in the social reality being studied. He must only ascertain the effect of their presence, combination and effective function. It is the philosopher who must be concerned with the justification of the validity and the value.... To deduce an epistemology from the sociology of knowledge would be as ill-fated as to link the fate of the sociology of knowledge to a particular philosophical position.... It is essential for the development of the sociology of knowledge that it learn to remain modest and renounce inordinate pretension.

I should also like to emphasize that in the following discussion of the five levels, I shall have to restrict the analysis to what is relevant to my earlier discussion of knowledge and the curriculum : I shall have to ignore most of the other very valuable ideas which emerge concerning teacher–pupil relationships and teaching-style.

Level 1 This is clearly derived from the Marxian view mentioned earlier in the chapter (p. 52), namely that education in a capitalist society is merely a 'tool of ruling class interest': education in a bourgeois society inevitably stresses competition, examining and selecting. Young wishes to avoid a simplistic acceptance of this view, however, which he claims is too general. Young prefers the approach suggested by the Italian Marxist Gramsci : 'Sociologists should raise the wider question of the relation between school knowledge and common sense knowledge, of how, as Gramsci suggests, knowledge available to certain groups becomes "school knowledge" or "educational" and that available to others does not' (Young, p. 28).

At this level, then, we are concerned with the more subtle aspects of inequality. Earlier writers such as Floud and Halsey had documented various kinds of inequalities in educational selection—for example, they were concerned with working-class opportunities of access to grammar schools, and achievement by working-class pupils in schools. An important development suggested by Young is that we should also be concerned with wider differences in access to knowledge, especially social class differences.

At this level Young is concerned with problems about the social distribution of knowledge (p. 31) :

Consideration of the assumption underlying the selection
and organisation of knowledge by those in positions of power
may be a fruitful perspective for raising sociological questions
about curriculum. We can make this more explicit by starting
with the assumptions that those in positions of power will
attempt to define what is to be taken as knowledge, how
accessible to different groups any knowledge is, and what are

the accepted relationships between different knowledge areas and between those who have access to them and make them available.

This suggestion is a valuable contribution to some current educational controversies. It calls into question the validity of such practices as streaming and such concepts as compensatory education (see also Bernstein, 1970).

Level 2 asks somewhat more searching questions. Whereas Level 1 was concerned with the social distribution of knowledge in society, Level 2 looks critically at knowledge itself: *what counts for knowledge in our society and how knowledge is stratified or differentially valued.* Level 2 is closely connected with Level 1 but with certain significant developments. Whereas Level 1 is concerned with the question of the social injustice involved in the social distribution of knowledge, Level 2 is concerned with evaluative judgments about different kinds of knowledge.

The term used for these questions is the stratification of knowledge, the fact that knowledge (which is distributed unequally) is also graded as 'high status', 'low status', etc. We have also to ask questions about *why* certain kinds of knowledge should be given a higher prestige than other kinds—why should a knowledge of dead languages such as Latin or Greek be more highly prestigious than Russian? Why should carpentry be of lower status than pottery? Level 2 is essentially concerned with the relative values put upon knowledge as opposed to the logical questions that might be raised about the divisions of knowledge (Level 3).

Young (p. 25) relates questions about the stratification of knowledge, or the differences in the prestige of certain subjects, to the problem of educational 'failure':

> We can usefully reformulate the problem in a similar way to that suggested by Cicourel and Kitsuse (1963) in their discussion of how official statistics on crime are produced, and ask what are the processes by which rates of educational success and failure come to be produced. We are then led to ask questions about the context and definition of success and how they are legitimized. In other words, the methods of assessment, selection and organisation of knowledge and the principles underlying them become our focus of study. The point is important because what is implied is that questions have to be raised about matters that have either not been considered important or have been tacitly accepted as 'given'. How does the education that poor working class children fail at come to be provided?

It is indeed surprising that such questions about the content of the curriculum have taken so long to emerge, and we should acknowledge our debt to Young and his contributors for raising them in this theoretical framework. Earlier sociologists, as Young points out, had made interesting comparative studies but little attempt had been made previously to apply these insights to the contemporary curriculum. For example, Weber (1952) had made an interesting study of the education of the Chinese literati or administrators. Weber pointed out that literati were selected to administer vast territories, even at times of civil unrest, on the basis of written examinations on classical literary texts. Weber noted the apparent discrepancy between the knowledge required to be an effective administrator and the very limited range of knowledge in which literati were educated. He also observed that the system tended to preserve the *status quo* in Chinese society, but he did not explore the possibility of those with non-bookish knowledge forming a competing power group.

Similarly, Wilkinson (1964) compared Weber's description with the classics-based, nineteenth-century public school curriculum. There is much work still to be done in applying this kind of Weberian analysis to contemporary education. Young, however, puts forward (p. 38) interesting suggestions along these lines about school knowledge today:

We ... suggest the dominant characteristics of high status knowledge, which we will hypothesise as the organising principles underlying academic curricula. These are literacy ... individualism ... abstractness ... and ... the unrelatedness of academic curricula, which refers to the extent to which they are 'at odds' with daily life and common experience.

Some difficulties now begin to emerge. The first is that the assumption seems to be made that the only reasons for labelling knowledge as high status or low status are social ones: the enormous amount of work which has been done by philosophers to justify the use of the term 'worthwhile' knowledge is ignored or dismissed without discussion. The second difficulty which emerges is that there appear to be internal inconsistencies in the argument: although the general message appears to be that such stratification of knowledge is unjustifiable, Esland, for example, puts forward his own (unargued) stratification of knowledge in terms of concrete and abstract, or common sense versus theoretical; in the midst of an attack on the Schools Council, he makes the following statement (Young, pp. 91-2):

The vocabularies of motive of this document [i.e. *Cross'd with*

Adversity] suggests a view of the child and the quality of his thinking as not only different, but deficient. His processes of nomization and meaning construction, the content and operation of his interpretational structures, are not considered. The way to get him to learn is to incorporate the familiar and the relevant into his curriculum, *thereby trivialising the knowledge which he can learn.* (Italics mine.)

Nevertheless, despite these two reservations, I would suggest that the thesis at Level 2 (together with Level 1) would still be generally acceptable to philosophers and to sociologists : useful questions are asked about the distribution of knowledge (Level 1) and the stratification of knowledge (Level 2). It is, however, foolish to ignore the possibility that there may well be important characteristics of certain kinds of knowledge which are not irrelevant to their inclusion in or exclusion from school curricula. My main criticism is, then, that Young's persuasive arguments in drawing our attention to some of the social factors in curriculum organization should not blind us to the fact that there may be other important factors as well as those he has dismissed : it is at least possible that some kinds of knowledge are superior in some meaningful way to other kinds of knowledge.

Level 3: Subject barriers are arbitrary and artificial This is in some ways a development of Level 2. Part of the questioning process about why certain kinds of knowledge are included in contemporary curricula gave rise to the question of subdividing knowledge into subject compartments. The implicit assumption seems to be that not only are 'subject barriers' arbitrary and artificial, but also that they often hinder rather than promote learning. It also seems to be suggesting that subjects are 'used' as a deliberate means of hindering learning in certain cases.

Young seems to move from a position of questioning the validity of subjects, to an assumption that they are merely social constructs, without, in the process, satisfactorily examining the case for subjects. Young's assumption seems to be that if the existence of subjects results in an unfair distribution of knowledge in society, then subjects should be abolished. Philosophical arguments are again turned aside without critical analysis (p. 23) :

The problem with this kind of critique (i.e. philosophical critique) is that it appears to be based on the absolutist conception of a set of distinct forms of knowledge which correspond closely to the traditional areas of the academic curriculum and thus justify, rather than examine, what are no more than the socio-historical constructs of the particular time. It is important to stress that it is not 'subjects' which Hirst recognises as the socially constructed ways that teachers organise knowledge, but forms of understanding, that it is claimed are necessarily distinct. The point I wish to make here is that unless such necessary distinctions or intrinsic logics are treated as problematic, philosophical criticism cannot examine the assumptions of academic curricula.

I would readily agree that we must treat the question of subjects and the forms of knowledge as problematic, and they are certainly regarded as problematic by other philosophers, but what is disturbing is Young's assumption that the battle has been won when we have simply fixed the battlefield. Much more detailed discussion is needed, both of the sociological evidence and of the philosophical arguments. Neither appear in *Knowledge and Control*. Gurvitch's advice has again been ignored—in particular his warning that 'one cannot assert that knowledge is a simple projection, or an epiphenomenon of social reality without undermining or denigrating it' (Gurvitch, p. 11). It may well be that there are important pedagogical and philosophical questions to be raised about Hirst's approach, for example, but it will not do simply to ignore and dismiss without analysis an established point of view. To take a parallel example, Ivan Illich (1973) has suggested that doctors have used their institutionalized positions to acquire too much power, that they sometimes do more harm than good, and that we might be better off without them; but this is very different indeed from going on to say that there is no such thing as medical knowledge. In other words, we have to distinguish between the harmful effects of institutionalization and the existence or non-existence of a connected body of knowledge. To return to education, if it is true that school subjects at present hinder the learning of some pupils, the solution may be to reorganize the teaching of those subjects—it does not necessarily follow that subjects are always bad or that they do not exist. Presumably there is plenty of scope here for empirical research—given that agreement can be reached about what knowledge is to be learnt.

In this connection it is again necessary to make a distinction between the work of Bernstein and that of Young and Esland. Bernstein's paper does not make any assumption about the validity, or otherwise, of subjects or forms of knowledge, but is limited to a sociological analysis of the classification and framing of knowledge.

Clearly it would be of great benefit if teachers were encouraged to re-think the place of their subjects in the whole curriculum, and also to question the validity of subjects in general; it would also be

an advance if teachers felt that even if subject barriers are justifi-
able, there is a need for inter-disciplinary links. But this change in
teachers' attitudes is likely to be hindered by sociologists simply
assuming that subjects have no validity rather than treating the
question as problematic.

Level 4: That all knowledge is socially constructed This level
is to some extent a link between sociology and phenomenology.
Phenomenology began as a philosophical movement and is often
identified with the work of the philosopher Husserl (1859-1938). In
recent years there has been a revival of interest in phenomenology,
which has been due partly to attempts by sociologists to apply
some aspects of phenomenology to their own discipline (see Filmer,
et al., 1972, and Pivcevic, 1972, for conflicting views about the success of this attempt). Phenomenology is concerned with problems
of human consciousness: not with the 'real' character of objects
but only with their status as phenomena in our consciousness. Part
of the phenomenological method of analysis is deliberately to make
oneself doubt common-sense beliefs—to suspend conventional
beliefs in order to get closer to 'pure consciousness', i.e. consciousness uncontaminated by what most people believe.

One of the attractions of phenomenology for sociologists who
were dissatisfied with sociological theory was that it provided (or
was thought to provide) an alternative to the positivist view of
sociology. Their criticism of positivist sociology was that it had
become a kind of 'natural science of society' which takes the
methods of physics as the model for social science, but that this
was unacceptable because people were, by their nature, different
from physical objects. Phenomenology would seem to cast doubt
not simply on the appropriateness of applying the methods of
physical science to studies of human beings, but also on some of the
assumptions behind physical science (Silverman, in Filmer, 1972,
p. 6):

the basis of science is the assumption of a world 'out there'
whose existence is independent of the processes through which
it is studied and understood. The world ... presents itself as
an essentially *preconstituted* field of objects which awaits
explication. Phenomenology, on the other hand, implies the
problematic character of this very availability of the world for
analysis.

In phenomenological sociology there is a tendency to stress the
view that 'the world' or 'reality' is 'socially constructed'. Part of
the difficulty here is to know exactly what is meant. If it means
that we see the world in certain ways *partly* because we have been
brought up to think in this way by the language and institutional-

ized beliefs of our culture, then this is little different from main-stream sociological theories of socialization. If, on the other hand, we are expected to accept the view that the *only* reason for possessing knowledge or beliefs are social then this is very different.

Thus one kind of ambiguity here is the *extent* to which the social construction of knowledge is supposed to apply. Marx and Mannheim appeared to exclude mathematics and some kinds of science from this generalization. Berger and Luckman are less clear on this point; but Young and Esland seem to be prepared to go the whole way and to generalize about *all* knowledge. Young clearly suggests (p. 77) that all the bodies of knowledge are socially constructed and subject to change, and by way of support, quotes C. W. Mills's statement that 'the rules of the game change with a shift in interest'. According to Young *all* kinds of truth and all rules for verification—including those of science—are simply institutionalized conventions. This version of the social construction of knowledge is also connected, in Young's writing, with social or cultural relativity, i.e. the idea that a view of reality is not right or wrong but 'relative', and that one view of reality is as valid as another (except presumably his own view of reality, which must in some way be regarded by Young as superior to other views of reality).

Young's chapter seems to imply that the *only* reasons for believing something are those determined by the social structure—probably the interests of those in power; but there is a very important difference between saying that social factors influence knowledge and that social factors determine knowledge, that is, that the social factors are the *only* factors involved. Failure to make this distinction makes Young's view, to say the least, simplistic. As Pring (1972) has pointed out, the fact that we happen to make distinctions in our culture between cats and dogs may be due to certain social conditions; the fact that we *can* distinguish between them has something to do with cats and dogs:

> The point of clarification therefore concerns the scope of the thesis. From the rather trivial points that all concepts are social and that all reality is mediated through concepts, is it being argued that reality is *nothing but* a social construction, and there are no other limiting features either in the nature of thought (picked out by philosophy) or in the nature of reality?

It may also be that what C. W. Mills is saying about truth and the changing forms of verification is very little different from the philosophical point made by Paul Hirst which will be considered in Chapter 5 (i.e. that different forms of knowledge have a number of distinguishing characteristics such as validation tests). Thus, there are serious criticisms to be made about Young's view of the social construction of reality and cultural relativity: first, it is not clear what is meant; second, if it means what it seems to mean, it is seriously inadequate—philosophical views of knowledge and reality other than the phenomenological should be considered (see Chapter 5). We must also know from Young and Esland where they think relativizing should stop—presumably it has to stop somewhere. Given that concepts are 'socially constructed' we need to know to what extent it is open to any group to reconstruct. Is it legitimate, according to Young and Esland, to reconstruct reality in such a way as to depart completely from the basic categories of thought from which they started? Young seems to jump from the social nature of concepts to the complete freedom of any individual (or group) to start afresh with no rules of organization of thought at all.

Level 5: Rationality itself is merely a convention This takes us even further away from credibility. From suggesting that all knowledge is socially constructed (and therefore arbitrary) it is only a short step to suggest that the criteria by which we decide on truth or falsehood are also socially constructed and could therefore be altered. Young (p. 5) again quotes C. W. Mills in support of his own view that our version of logic or rational thinking should be seen as 'sets of social conventions'. Young claims that 'Mills goes on to suggest that the rules of logic, whether practical or academic, are conventional, and will be shaped and selected in accordance with the purpose of the discourse or the intentions of the enquiries'.

Thus rationality itself is called into question, certainly by Young, less certainly by Mills for reasons which I suggested above, i.e. that there is at least a suspicion that Mills is saying no more than that the rules for conceptualization and verification are different from time to time and different according to the context (or in philosophical terms, according to the form of knowledge which is being used). Hirst himself has made clear that forms of knowledge are not static but that their criteria do develop and change *to some extent*. Mills's statement seems to have been interpreted by Young to mean that the criteria and forms of verification are not absolute but conventional and relative, and that our views of rationality are also socially determined. Similarly, Kuhn is cited in a way which is questionable. In *The Structure of Scientific Revolutions* Kuhn (1970a) suggests that science is not a cumulative process of steady progress by means of scientific method, but a much more complicated series of scientific traditions, or paradigms, which are periodically overthrown by revolutionary new paradigms. Kuhn seems to suggest that neither adherence to the old paradigms of 'normal science' nor their overthrow is *completely* explicable in

terms of scientific rationality, since scientific discovery can sometimes be related to social and psychological factors rather than to
scientific methodology. This interesting, but some would say oversimplified, account of changes in science is, however, taken up
by Esland (Young, 1971, pp. 80-2) to cast serious doubt on the
validity of scientific thinking, and even rationality itself. A number
of clarifications are needed at this stage: first, sociologists should
heed Gurvitch's warning and not jump from saying that because
social factors *can* be related to knowledge in some way, that
knowledge is *merely* a social construct. There is nothing in Kuhn
to justify that. Secondly, the views of Kuhn have themselves been
challenged by other scientists (see Clarke, 1973, for a brief discussion of the controversy). For example, Toulmin (1970) has
continued to argue that most progress in science is evolutionary
rather than revolutionary in character, and Popper (1970) also
questions whether Kuhn's distinction between normal and revolutionary science is a valid and appropriate one; for Popper *all* science
is essentially critical rather than 'conventional' or dogmatic, and
Kuhn's description of a 'normal scientist' is simply a badly educated
scientist. But even for Kuhn, science is clearly regarded as a rational
pursuit even if scientists themselves are sometimes less than completely rational. Paradigms come and go but all this takes place
within a general framework of scientific methodology. In a careful
defence of his position (Kuhn, 1970b) Kuhn explicitly rejects the
idea that rationality itself is open to question: 'No process essential
to scientific development can be labelled "irrational" without vast
violence to the term.' It would be fair to describe Kuhn as a
'historical relativist' (Popper, 1970) but not as an irrationalist.

If rationality itself is called into question by Young we also
have to ask how this can be done without employing rational
methods of enquiry. To ask questions, to criticize, is to use reason,
and it is difficult to see how it could be otherwise. It seems to me
that Young, *et al.*, are guilty of self-contradiction: they take great
pains to ask questions which elsewhere they seem to say have no
'real' meaning. But it is not only the philosophical or logical aspects
of their position which have been neglected. Throughout their
discussions much is made of the *differences* between cultures in
their interpretations of reality, but what is really so impressive
about anthropological or ethno-linguistic studies is not the differences between cultures but the amazing *similarities* in language
and logic. Nowhere in *Knowledge and Control*, or in the writings of
C. W. Mills, is there an example of a culture whose mode of rationality is unrecognizable to us. Similarly, as Chomsky has pointed out,
what is interesting about the structure of different languages is
their basic *similarity* of structure, not the comparatively insigni-

ficant minor differences. Thus, the sociological evidence and linguistic evidence has also been neglected by Young; the psychological and epistemological work of Piaget has also been virtually ignored: for example, the fact that the application of Piaget's experiments in different cultures have shown similarities in mental development rather than different kinds of logic. Nowhere in *Knowledge and Control* is Piaget's work on epistemology and the structure of knowledge mentioned; nowhere is Kohlberg's cross-cultural work on moral development referred to.

The tendency to ignore established views and evidence is perhaps the worst feature of this approach. It would appear that Young and some of his colleagues are so fascinated by the 'interpretive paradigm' that they impatiently discard other views without adequate examination, so that the result is often an interpretation which is oversimplified and naïve. Nell Keddie's work (1973; and in Young, 1971) sometimes comes into this category: her contribution to *Knowledge and Control* is very interesting and especially welcome as an empirical contribution to the discussion of 'educational failure'. Much of the data discussed is interesting, and she establishes a convincing case for the importance of teachers' attitudes and expectations in influencing pupils' behaviour and performance. But two important factors are ignored: first, the *possibility* that 'intelligence' might still be an important factor—perhaps some of the materials were too difficult for the pupils. Second, the possibility that some children's home background would handicap them in school even if all the teachers were 'perfect' (according to Keddie's criteria). Keddie's analysis of teachers' behaviour is useful but because she ignores other—possibly relevant —factors, it could result in a view of 'teacher-failure' just as deterministic as the conventional one of 'pupil-failure'. Similarly in *Tinker, Tailor ... The Myth of Cultural Deprivation*, Keddie argues that working-class children should not be seen in terms of a 'vacuum ideology', i.e. as lacking culture simply because they are different from middle-class teachers. In order to demonstrate the 'myth of cultural deprivation', she discusses articles by seven authors writing about groups with cultural *differences* who might be seen as culturally *deprived* by the anthropologically naïve. Unfortunately, not one of the seven papers is directly related in any way to English working-class children, so their value to her main argument is limited. In addition there is a logical flaw in her main argument which might be summarized as follows:

1. Many examples of cultural difference have been regarded as cultural deprivation;
2. there is evidence to show that some of those groups have a rich and complicated culture;

3. therefore cultural deprivation does not exist.

Surely it would be better to argue on logical rather than empirical grounds—that no child could possibly be culturally deprived unless brought up isolated from people, since all people living together have a culture. Simply to quote a few examples of 'rich' but mis-understood cultures does not establish the relativist thesis that one culture is just as good as another. What also need to be discussed are the criteria by which we can judge cultures. Finally another implication in the general argument needs questioning: given that cultural deprivation cannot (normally) exist, does it follow that there is no such thing as an impoverished environment?

Michael F. D. Young and his colleagues have raised some impor-tant questions, especially at Levels 1, 2 and possibly 3. But these questions are likely to be much more helpful in assisting teachers revise their pedagogy or teaching-methods rather than to reform the curriculum. Most of the direct benefit from *Knowledge and Control* will be to make teachers question certain aspects of their teaching-style and the relationship with pupils. Because of the con-fusion of the valid questions of Levels 1 and 2 with the increasingly mysterious dogma of Levels 3, 4 and 5, the possibility of reform is likely to give way to despair—if all knowledge is of equal worth then why have schools at all? If rationality is relative is there any point in talking to each other, let alone writing books?

Summary

To return to my main theme, i.e. the problem of planning a curri-culum, the help gained from Marx, Mannheim, Berger and Luckman and the authors of *Knowledge and Control* is in the form of highly significant questions rather than answers. First, there are social factors to be unravelled in such questions as what counts as educational knowledge, and why? Secondly, what changes should be made in school curricula and why? Thirdly, how can curricula be planned so that pupils will have equal access to knowledge (even if they differ in achievement)?

It is important to realize that curriculum planning will involve not only sociological enquiry but philosophical and psychological research as well. The sociology of knowledge cannot supersede all the other disciplines.

We need also to distinguish between the use made of those aspects of the so-called interpretive paradigm (Levels 1 and 2) which are very useful, and the phenomenological view of knowledge which does not seem to get us very far in curriculum planning. The criticism of positivistic sociology is helpful but we are not offered constructive alternatives.

69

5

Knowledge
and curriculum planning

Education is concerned with the transmission of culture to the next generation; curriculum planning is concerned with the selection of knowledge for transmission and the principles by which the selection is made. I have re-stated the argument in this way to emphasize the crucial position of knowledge in the educational process—a point which tends to be obscured by some kinds of sociological discussion. We are therefore back to the position of examining the kinds of knowledge available for selection and the criteria by which selection may be made.

Schools and the transmission of knowledge

I should like to begin by taking up one point from Chapter 4: Bernstein's division of knowledge into common-sense knowledge and non-common-sense knowledge, and his suggestion that schools are concerned with various kinds of non-common-sense knowledge. If we mean by common sense the kinds of knowledge and view of reality which are 'picked-up' informally rather than learned systematically this is a very useful distinction. If informal induction by family and peer group into common-sense, everyday reality were regarded as sufficient, then clearly schools would be quite unnecessary. But unlike many pre-industrial and pre-literate societies, our culture has become so complex that informal learning is insufficient for at least two reasons: the wide range of knowledge (and its rapid growth) which is regarded as necessary for a general understanding of our culture; and the need for education to lay the foundation for specialized vocational training. This is part of the tension which Raymond Williams referred to, between the three kinds of educators: 'the public educators, the industrial trainers, and the old humanists' (1961, p. 163).

70

Before proceeding with this analysis it would be as well to emphasize one point. In accepting the useful distinction between common-sense knowledge and school knowledge, I am not suggesting that they are completely different or that there is no connection between them. I would suggest that school knowledge or academic knowledge is an extension and refinement of common-sense reality. If it sometimes appears that school knowledge has no connection with reality then this is due to poor teaching (as Douglas Barnes, 1969, has shown us). There is, in my opinion, no justification for making rigid distinctions between discipline-centred and child-centred learning. Those curriculum theorists who advocate situation-centred learning (Freire, 1971; Robinsohn, 1969) do not contest the importance of 'disciplines'—they argue for making them relevant to the 'situations' of the majority, and I would agree completely with their emphasis.

The history of mankind is the long story of men interacting with the environment, interpreting the interaction in various ways and acquiring a degree of mastery over the environment. The accumulation of many generations' interactions with the physical environment (and with other people) is called knowledge. Each generation thus has the three-fold task of efficiently learning the knowledge acquired by previous generations, adding to it or modifying the interpretations, and finally passing this revised knowledge on to the next generation. If a culture is reasonably simple everything may be regarded as common sense, but as skills and technology become more and more complex, more specialized learning becomes essential.

The paragraph above conveys what might be described as the anthropological or cultural view of knowledge. Let me now approach the question from a slightly different angle. The key to human learning is the power to generalize: every incident of experience is unique, but if we regarded all events as unique, learning would be impossible. We only learn by seeing relationships, and in order to see relationships, we need concepts. Concepts are formed by making particular incidents or things, into classes: we conceptualize by classifying. Without this ability to classify, conceptualize and generalize we would be imprisoned forever in the 'blooming, buzzing confusion' that William James referred to.

Knowledge and the disciplines

But thinking does not stop at the point of making single concepts or single generalizations. Just as we link unique events by analysis to form concepts, so we link some concepts together and exclude others to form conceptual systems. Part of the learning process is concerned with seeing which kinds of concepts and generalizations are related to each other or fit together, and which do not. For example, quite young children learn that it is regarded as inappropriate to talk of a 'naughty lawn-mower'—the word 'naughty', and others conveying moral disapproval or approval, have to be collocated with some kind of intention, whereas lawn-mower belongs to a technology-set of inanimate, non-feeling objects. That kind of distinction in language is acquired early on in the world of everyday reality, but slightly more complex examples would take us into the kind of conceptual network which we call *disciplines*.

There are also other explanations of why knowledge may be usefully subdivided into disciplines which may have some relevance to the problem of organizing and selecting knowledge in the process of curriculum planning. They are all related to the basic point I have made above, but the justification of each emphasizes different aspects of the process of knowledge acquisition. If we ask the question 'Why disciplines, or why different forms of knowledge?', I suggest that there are four kinds of answer which we should examine:

1. Because reality is like that.
2. Because different sorts of questions are being asked.
3. Because children develop in that way.
4. Because disciplines promote more economical learning.

(1) Disciplines justified in terms of the nature of reality A naïve, realist point of view is that the world exists 'out there', with certain fixed characteristics, and man's search for knowledge is a simple cumulative process of gradually uncovering more and more of 'Nature's secrets'. This might also be described as the man-in-the-street or common-sense view of reality. Unfortunately there are a number of difficulties in accepting such a simple picture: even in those branches of science concerned with the physical world, it is increasingly difficult to regard knowledge as uncovering 'the truth': it is a much more complex process of puzzle-solving within theoretical frameworks created by scientists (see the discussion of Kuhn, in Chapter 4); in the social sciences the 'human contribution' by way of theories and ideologies is even greater. Thus 'reality' is a combination of man-made and natural phenomena: 'The form of a statement of a scientific hypothesis and its use to express a general proposition is a human device; what is due to Nature are the observable facts which refute or fail to refute the hypothesis ...' (Braithwaite, 1952, quoted by Lakatos). In other words, facts do not 'speak for themselves', they only 'speak' in some kind of meaningful context—which is always man-made. The extent to which reality

is man-made or 'natural' is a point which sharply divides philosophers and curriculum theorists. Phenix (1962, pp. 273-80), for example, is firmly committed to the 'realist' position, i.e. that there is a real objective world which we gradually discover, classify and reduce to meaningful knowledge.

The priority and primacy of the disciplines in education are greatly buttressed by a realistic view of knowledge, as opposed to a nominalistic one. In realism it is asserted that concepts and theories disclose the real nature of things, while in nominalism it is affirmed that the structure of thought is a matter of human convention. Academic and educational nominalists believe that experience can be categorised and concepts organised in endless ways, according to inclination and decision and for the convenience of individuals and society. Furthermore, it is held, scholars can choose their own special ways of organising knowledge and educators can choose other ways, the differences corresponding to the disparity and purposes in the two groups. Thus arise the supposed contrasts between the logic of the disciplines and the psycho-logic of the educative process.

Such nominalism is rejected in the realistic view here proposed. From a realistic standpoint, nominalism is epistemologically impious and pedagogically disastrous, a source of internecine strife and intellectual estrangement. There is a logos of being which it is the office of reason to discover. The structure of things is revealed, not invented, and it is the business of enquiry to open that structure to general understanding through the formation of appropriate concepts and theories. Truth is rich and varied, but it is not arbitrary. The nature of things is given, not chosen, and if man is to gain insight he must employ the right concepts and methods. Only by obedience to the truth thus discovered can he learn or teach.

In short, authentic disciplines are at one and the same time approximations to the given orders of reality and disclosures of the paths by which persons may come to realise truth in their own being, which is simply to say that the disciplines are the sole proper source of the curriculum.

The nominalist position—or at least one version of it—has already been considered critically in Chapter 4. It is unnecessary to go over this argument again at this stage. Phenix has stated the realist position in an extreme form—some would say an extravagant form. Nevertheless there are many who would agree with him.

73

Unfortunately Phenix's statement is not only extreme but also does less than justice to the case for disciplines. What should be contrasted with nominalism is the view that the way in which we have come to conceptualize the world *does* eventually get at the real essence of things even if our methods of classification are developed for a variety of reasons, including some social or political ones. Another fault of the Phenix statement is that it seems to suggest that the disciplines have already reached a stage of perfection—it assumes that we already know what all the right concepts and methods are. But the rejection of the extreme kind of realism put forward by Phenix does not mean that we have to take up an equally extreme kind of nominalist position: a *via media* is much more fruitful. In other words, the kind of nominalism which suggests that classifications are mere conventions does not necessarily cut out the existence of meaningful constraints on mere conventions, i.e. given that one could classify things differently for different purposes, there are still limits imposed by the nature of the universe. There is something about the world that both makes classification possible and yet prevents some kinds of classification. There are limits which are imposed not by man's traditions or conventions but by the nature of reality. These kinds of distinction may be very important for curriculum planning because questions about disciplines relate to questions about purposes or the questions being asked (see 2 below), whereas for an extreme realist (or essentialist) the questions being asked are, logically, irrelevant, i.e. the 'real world' simply 'exists' out there, and all we have to do is find out about it. It seems much more likely that our classifications of reality expressed in the disciplines are partly conventional (i.e. they could be rearranged) and partly 'real'.

(2) Different disciplines ask different questions   This leads us to the second argument in support of basing a curriculum on disciplines, namely that the various disciplines are asking different kinds of questions and making different kinds of statement. Thus the 'same' landscape will be seen in different ways by a geologist, who might be interested in the rock formations, a historian who analyses its importance in the result of a significant battle, or an artist who wants to paint it. Different kinds of question are being asked, which leads to different kinds of methods of procedure and different end-results. It is clearly important that *at some stage* (see 3 below) pupils should come to see the differences between disciplines, and the curriculum is an important means of organizing this. Unfortunately, in the past, schools have often only succeeded in differentiating between disciplines at the cost of ignoring the relationships between them.

(3) Disciplines and the nature of human learning The third argument in favour of basing a curriculum on disciplines concerns the view that *children learn in this way.* This argument might be closely connected with the work of Piaget, which cannot adequately be summarized here. The last chapter of *The Development of Logical Thinking from Childhood to Adolescence* is extremely relevant in this connection, as is his later book *Psychology and Epistemology.* Piaget's work certainly provides some support for the view that the process by which children classify experience is not simply the result of the social norms of the culture they happen to be born into: there is something in human mental structure that facilitates certain kinds of conceptualization. There is evidence about a human predisposition to categorize in certain ways not only in the fields of mathematics and science, but also in moral development (Kohlberg, 1964), and also the 'deep structure' of linguistic categories referred to by Chomsky (1966) in his work on children's acquisition of language. A child's development is neither simply a matter of socialization into cultural norms nor is it a question of automatic maturation. It is a very complex process of the interaction of a developing child with the social and physical environment. R. S. Peters in *Ethics and Education* (p. 49) has very clearly made the link between the child and the social world:

> In the history of philosophy Kant rightly achieved fame for outlining this structure of concepts and categories by means of which order is imposed on the flux of experience; this he attributed to an active reason at work in the experience of all individuals. Later on, in the early part of the twentieth century, the psychologist Piaget, much influenced by Kant, laboriously mapped the stages at which these concepts and categories develop. But neither of these thinkers speculated about the extent to which the development of mind is the product of initiation into public traditions enshrined in a public language.

There is certainly a good deal of evidence to justify the view that children do have predispositions to categorize reality in certain basic ways. But the emergence of knowledge is the result of a complex set of interactions between a unique individual (who possesses certain psychological predispositions to classify experience), the 'real world', and the set of interpretations of the real world which we refer to as culture. The basic predispositions referred to, do not correspond exactly with our own cultural constructs—the disciplines or forms of knowledge. There is, however, enough evidence to suggest that children's understanding of reality will be enhanced by being able to make, at some stage in their development, those distinctions which correspond to some extent with 'disciplines' however defined. This does *not* mean, of course, that we should necessarily organize the whole curriculum on disciplines or subjects. But the discipline factor should not be ignored. On the one hand, Piaget has described certain very general, logical features of thought which are characteristic of all the disciplines, and which might be best thought of as pre-disciplinary in curriculum terms. On the other hand, the features of particular disciplines are developed and acquired socially—but this social development is constrained to some extent by 'deep structures', i.e. certain mental predispositions, shared to some extent by all human beings, to develop thought in certain ways. Nevertheless there are important distinctions to be made here, between the logical ordering of a particular discipline and the 'natural' psychological development of the child. It is certainly not my intention to play down the importance of the purely social factors in classifying and ordering reality.

(4)   Disciplines and efficient learning   Finally I should like to consider the fourth argument in favour of basing learning on disciplines or forms of knowledge—the suggestion that *learning by means of disciplines is made easier or more efficient*. This point about the psychology of learning is distinct from the logic of the structure of disciplines, considered briefly above in 2 and 3, but there are important points of overlap between the arguments. This psychological argument has been put forward by such curriculum theorists as Phenix (1962) to support his more philosophical views:

> The test of a good discipline is whether or not it simplifies understanding. When a field of study only adds new burdens and multiplies complexities, it is not properly called a discipline. Likewise, when a real discipline in certain directions begins to spawn concepts and theories which on balance are a burden and hindrance to insight, in those areas it degenerates into undisciplined thinking. One of the greatest barriers to progress in learning is the failure to catch the vision of simplicity which the disciplines promise.

Such arguments ought, however, to be related to empirical enquiry. There has been a good deal of speculation and discussion along these lines but rather less research. Much of what research has been done stems from the ideas of Bruner: 'Every subject has a structure, a rightness, a beauty. It is this structure that provides the underlying simplicity of things, and it is by learning its nature that we come to appreciate the intrinsic meaning of a subject' (J. S. Bruner, 'Structures in Learning', in Hass *et al.*, 1970, p. 314). Bruner has also given examples and evidence to support this view of the importance of structure in learning: 'Grasping the structure of a subject is understanding it in a way that permits many other things to be related to it meaningfully. To learn structure, in short, is to learn how things are related' (*The Process of Education*, p.7).

Chapter 2 of the same book is devoted to 'The Importance of Structure' and gives examples mainly from mathematics and science. In a later book *Toward a Theory of Instruction* Bruner also includes some interesting examples to illustrate the importance and efficiency of structure in the learning process, and Bruner also boldly ventures away from the 'safe' disciplines of mathematics and science into the more controversial field of the social sciences. In his chapter on 'Man, A Course of Study' Bruner suggests a conceptual structure for the course. He suggests that the social sciences are based on three fundamental questions: 'What is human about human beings? How did they get that way? How can they be made more so?' In pursuit of these questions Bruner suggests (1966, p. 75) five humanizing forces as the underlying structure of the course: 'tool-making, language, social organisation, the management of man's prolonged childhood, and man's urge to explain the world.'

Other social studies curriculum projects have chosen different questions and different key concepts (see the Liverpool Social Science Project, for example), but the point to be made is that *some* structure is needed in order to learn about man if we are not to accumulate a mere collection of bits of disconnected information. Much of the criticism of school social studies has in fact been based on its unstructured, unsystematic, undisciplined content. Some kind of sequence and structure is needed in this area even if the structure is much more arbitrary than the structure of disciplines such as mathematics and science. Similarly, Ausubel (1959, p. 79), in a critical review of some exaggerated versions of child-centred education and informal learning, appeals for more structure:

Even more important, however, is the realisation that in older children, once a sufficient number of basic concepts are consolidated, new concepts are primarily abstracted from verbal rather than from concrete experience. Hence in secondary school it may be desirable to reverse both the sequence and the relative balance between abstract concepts and supportive data. There is good reason for believing, therefore, that much of the time presently spent in cook-book laboratory exercises in the sciences could be much more advantageously employed in formulating precise definitions, making explicit verbal distinctions between concepts, generalising from hypothetical situations, and in other ways.

Whether or not these examples of discipline structures are 'real', or imposed by the culture, seems to be less important than the fact that they are necessary for efficient learning (Bruner, 1972, pp. 16-17):

> The disciplines of learning represent not only codified knowledge but ways of thought, habits of mind, implicit assumptions, short cuts, and styles of humor that never achieve explicit statement. Concentrations of these ways of thought probably account for the phenomenal productivity in ideas and men of, say, the Cavendish Laboratory under Rutherford or Copenhagen under Bohr. For these ways of thought keep knowledge lively, keep the knower sensitive to opportunity and anomaly. I draw attention to this matter, for studies in the history of knowledge suggest that deadening and banalization are also characteristics of knowledge once it becomes codified.

How many disciplines?

If the suggestion that education should be based not only on knowledge but on the separate disciplines or forms of knowledge is accepted, it is necessary to see exactly what these disciplines are. There is some variety in the kind of responses given to this question —the answers range from three to eight or more categories. But this apparent contradiction may be less disturbing than appears at first sight—as usual in such discussion and in such classifications there is a difficulty of defining exactly what is meant by discipline. Considerable work has been done in this field by the American curriculum theorist J. J. Schwab (1964). Schwab puts forward four bases for classifying disciplines: first, the *subject matter*; second, the characteristics of the members of the particular *community of scholars*; third, the syntax they use, i.e. their *methods* of procedure and modes of enquiry; and finally the *kinds of knowledge* they are aiming at. Clearly such a four-fold system of classifying is likely to produce scholars working in disciplines which are partly 'real' and partly 'man-made'. There are real distinctions but the actual number of discrete areas or communities of scholars is *to some extent* fluid and the barriers arbitrary. Another distinction which should be made is the difference between disciplines and forms of knowledge. Hirst, for example, would use many of the same criteria in determining forms of knowledge as Schwab uses in his discussion of disciplines, but some of Hirst's forms would include several disciplines (e.g. Hirst's natural science form of knowledge would include a very large number of disciplines such as chemistry, physics, botany, biochemistry, etc.). There does not seem to me to be serious disagreement between Hirst and Schwab.

Schwab (1962), for example, puts forward the view that there are three *kinds of* disciplines. He refers to these as the investigative disciplines (roughly mathematics and the natural sciences), the appreciative disciplines (the arts), and finally the decisive disciplines (the social sciences). Peterson (1960), on the other hand, recommends a curriculum of general education based on four main modes of intellectual activity : the logical, the empirical, the moral and the aesthetic.

H. S. Broudy (1962) has developed a curriculum plan based on five groups of disciplines which he derives from the theoretical work of Tykociner.

1. Bodies of knowledge that serve as symbolic tools of thinking, communication and learning. These include the language of ordinary discourse, of logic, of quantity, and of art.
2. Bodies of knowledge that systematise basic facts and their relations. These disciplines (the sciences) give us a way of speaking and thinking about the world and everything in it; a way structured by the conceptual system that characterises each discipline.
3. Bodies of knowledge that organise information along the routes of cultural development. History, biography and evolutionary studies serve this purpose by giving some kind of order to the past.
4. Bodies of knowledge that project future problems and attempt to regulate the activities of the social order. Tykociner cites agriculture, medicine, technology, and national defence as examples of the former, and political science, jurisprudence, economics, and management as examples of the latter. We have also developed sciences to guide dissemination of knowledge, e.g. education, mass communication, journalism, library science, custodianship of records and relics.
5. The integrative and inspirational disciplines which create syntheses or value schema in the form of philosophies, theologies, and works of art.

Perhaps the best-known work on the structure and organization of knowledge in England is that of Paul Hirst, which was referred to in Chapter 2. Hirst states that all knowledge that man has achieved can be seen to be differentiated into a number of 'logically distinct domains or forms'. Hirst suggests that knowledge is possible only because of the use of patterns of related concepts in terms of which our experience is intelligible (Hirst in Tibble, 1966, p. 43):

That there are distinct forms within knowledge can be seen by the logical analysis of the whole domain. These forms can

79

be distinguished from each other in three inter-related ways. First, within the domain there are distinct types of concepts that characterise different types of knowledge.... Second, these concepts occur within different networks whose relationships determine what meaningful propositions can be made.... Third, the domains can be distinguished by the different types of test they involve for the truth or validity of propositions.

According to Hirst there are about seven forms of knowledge:

1. Mathematics and formal logic.
2. The physical sciences.
3. The human sciences, including history.
4. Moral understanding.
5. The religious form of knowledge.
6. Philosophy.
7. Aesthetics.

(See pages 16-19 for a further discussion of Hirst.)

Finally we come to another American point of view—that of Philip Phenix, whose book *The Realms of Meaning* (1964) has been very influential both in America and to some extent in this country. According to Phenix, education ought to be concerned with engendering *essential meanings*, and the curriculum should be planned with that end in view. Unlike many other curriculum theorists, however, Phenix does not base his entire division of knowledge on 'rationality'. His work is significantly different from Hirst's in this respect. Phenix contrasts the ability of human beings to derive meaning from other kinds of experience. According to Phenix the curriculum should be planned to pay particular attention to realms of meaning and meaninglessness. Phenix maps out six hierarchical realms of meaning, which may be associated with certain disciplines as follows (they are numbered in order of increasing complexity):

	The Realms of Meaning	*The Disciplines*
1.	Symbolics	Language, logic, mathematics, symbols in art.
2.	Empirics	Physical and social sciences.
3.	Aesthetics	Literature, music, art.
4.	Synnoetics	Literature, philosophy, history, psychology, theology.
5.	Ethics and morality	Parts of philosophy and theology.
6.	Synoptics	Philosophy, religion, history.

R. C. Whitfield has suggested in *Disciplines of the Curriculum* (1971) a means by which Phenix's theoretical work could be converted into a curriculum and even a timetable.

What all the above theorists have in common is much more

important than the differences between them. First of all they agree that disciplines are distinguished from each other not only by their content, subject matter or substantive form, but also by the rules, concepts, and methods of validation. Secondly, they agree that education should be concerned with learning about the differences between disciplines and also the relations between disciplines, i.e. the similarities between disciplines as well as the discipline boundaries (Peterson, 1960):

> They must have time and guidance in which to see that what is a proof in mathematics they pursue on Tuesday is not the same thing as a proof in history, which follows on Wednesday; that the truth of George Eliot or Joseph Conrad is not the same thing as the truths of Mendel or Max Planck; and yet that there are similarities as well as differences.

Hirst also argues along similar lines in Schools Council *Working Paper No. 12*. Thirdly, the theorists seem to be agreed that education should include an understanding of all the disciplines. The concept of the educated man is closely connected with an appreciation of the full range of the different kinds of knowledge and educative experiences.

Thus we are provided with two important criteria for curriculum planning: the principle of adequate *coverage* of the disciplines, and secondly the importance of achieving adequate *balance* between the disciplines. If education in schools is concerned with the transmission of a general understanding of the world and a general basis for later vocational specialization, then care should be taken in the construction of school curricula to ensure that important kinds of knowledge are not neglected or ignored and also that too much specialization in one area does not take place at the expense of other areas.

I want to argue that when we talk about a common culture, the central area for concern is connected with the forms of knowledge, or realms of meaning or disciplines. This is the major part of our common culture. Sub-cultural or regional differences are very important and should not be neglected, but as far as schools are concerned the first task is to work out a means of transmitting the public forms of knowledge which comprise our national, and to some extent, our international culture. The principles by which we can organize this central knowledge into a curriculum will be considered in the next chapter.

Summary

In this chapter, I have argued that education is largely concerned with those aspects of culture referred to as knowledge. Knowledge is not a unified whole but consists of logically different ways of enquiring into, understanding or experiencing 'reality'. The extent to which these forms of knowledge are objectively 'real' or are social constructs (in so far as this is a meaningful distinction) is less important than the fact of their usefulness in the learning process. The exact number of disciplines that should be included, or where the boundaries happen to be drawn, is of less importance than the necessity for pupils to be given *some* kind of structure in the learning process. This does *not* mean, of course, that inter-disciplinary work is of no importance: the exact relationship between subjects, disciplines and inter-disciplinary work on problems has been generally neglected, at a theoretical level, in curriculum planning. Nevertheless, there are a number of important arguments in favour of the structure of disciplines as a basis for curriculum organization. These arguments, which are often ignored in discussions of this subject are: first, that to some extent reality is made more meaningful by means of disciplines, secondly that the different disciplines are important because they look at reality in different ways, thirdly, that there is *some* relationship between disciplines and human mental structure, and finally, that there is evidence that discipline-structures facilitate learning.

It would be quite wrong, however, to see this chapter, in isolation from the rest of the book, as an argument in favour of a 'discipline-centred' curriculum. I would agree very much with Robinsohn (1968) that the separation of educationists into the 'illicit triad' of child-centred, society-centred and discipline-centred hardly applies at the level of situations and aims. We have to identify situations and functions of the individual *in* society. To master these situations he will need knowledge. My suggestion is that disciplines should be used in planning a curriculum, not that the curriculum should be discipline-centred.

6

A common culture curriculum

Disciplines: public forms of knowledge

If we agree that education is concerned with the transmission of knowledge (broadly defined), then a common culture curriculum must be primarily concerned with public forms of knowledge, or knowledge which can be made generally available by means of established disciplines. Whether we use the term 'forms of knowledge' or 'disciplines' or 'realms of meaning' may have some implications for how knowledge is structured and organized within the school, but the differences in practice are likely to be small. The real point to be established is that the organization of the school curriculum must be expressed within some kind of convention or framework which is reasonably clear and unambiguous. As Stenhouse (1970) has pointed out, one advantage of discussing curriculum in terms of disciplines is that identifiable standards are built into the structure, thus avoiding the need for the search for detailed and specific objectives which tend to be unworkable and unrealistic. A discipline can be thought of not only in terms of the kind of knowledge covered, but also in terms of the methods and rules of procedure regarded as valid by the practitioners—the 'community of scholars'. Thus, for example, it might be argued that an English teacher does not need a detailed list of objectives to be attained at the end of a term's work on Hamlet: he will be able to judge success and failure, or 'good' and 'bad' work, according to standards accepted by those who have made a study of literature. Standards will differ from discipline to discipline and in some cases may stress the content as much as the methods.

Disciplines but not subjects

This will mean that schools should concentrate on the transmission of knowledge, but not necessarily in the form of the traditional array of school subjects associated with the grammar school curriculum. Some of those who argue in favour of a curriculum based on 'the disciplines' are guilty of merely rationalizing their desire to preserve the *status quo* in the form of a grammar school pattern with or without some minor modifications. I should like to emphasize that there are very important differences between most grammar school curricula and a curriculum carefully planned on a basis of disciplines, forms of knowledge or realms of meaning. The traditional grammar school curriculum is not adequate for the so-called academic pupils in the top 20 per cent or so of the ability range, and it is certainly not suitable for the rest of the population.

There are at least two major criticisms to be made about the traditional grammar school pattern : the first concerns inadequate *coverage* of the forms of knowledge; the second concerns *balance*. There are important gaps in the pattern of subjects offered by most grammar schools and comprehensive schools—for example, social science and moral education have received too little time and attention. Secondly, the balance of the curriculum is distorted by far too much and too early specialization.

The main reason for these two criticisms is that the traditional secondary school syllabus is not discipline-based but *subject*-based. The trouble with curriculum planning based on subjects is that there are simply too many of them. As there are about 400 possible subjects to choose from, a selection is likely to be arbitrary, incomplete and resistant to change. Another possibility is that since no attempt can be made to cover the whole range of subjects, there is no reason why some subjects should not be dropped at an early stage in order to permit specialization in others. This process of arbitrary and narrow selection of subjects, combined with a high degree of specialization, reaches a climax in the English sixth form, the curriculum of which has for a long time been recognized as thoroughly unsatisfactory by most educationists. It has, however, shown itself to be a very difficult structure to change—witness the failure of the 'Agreement to Broaden the Curriculum' in the 1960s and also the successive attempts by the Schools Council to improve the balance and coverage of the sixth form curriculum. One of the reasons for this series of failures is that the sixth form curriculum has been examined separately from lower and middle school curricula. What is really needed is a re-examination of the secondary curriculum as a whole, and a move away from subjects to *disciplines* or 'faculties' to use the term adopted by some reforming secondary schools.

Two further qualifications need to be stressed at this point. The first is that a curriculum based on disciplines does not rule out the possibility of inter-disciplinary work: all the advocates of discipline-based curricula referred to in Chapter 5 stressed the importance of pupils understanding the nature of the overlap between disciplines, and the links between them as well as the differences. Secondly, there is no reason why a curriculum based on disciplines should not be related to the children's own experience and interests (or situations, to use the term preferred by Robinsohn, 1969). The fact that so much so-called academic teaching of subjects does tend to neglect children's everyday knowledge (see Barnes, 1969), is a condemnation of traditional pedagogy or teaching-method rather than the disciplines themselves as a basis of the curriculum.

Curriculum planning: five stages of selection

The problem of selecting from all the knowledge available still remains; I have suggested elsewhere (Lawton, 1973) that a useful method of setting about the task of curriculum planning is to make use of a flow chart something like Figure 1:

FIGURE I

Stage 1

> Philosophical questions
> (cultural universals):
> e.g., aims of education
> worthwhile knowledge etc.

Stage 2

> Sociological questions
> (cultural variables):
> e.g.,the kind of society
> we have/we want etc.

Stage 3

> Selection from Culture

Stage 4

> Psychological questions
> and theories:
> .e.g.,of learning
>   instruction
>   development etc.

Stage 5

> Curriculum organized
> in stages, sequence etc.

85

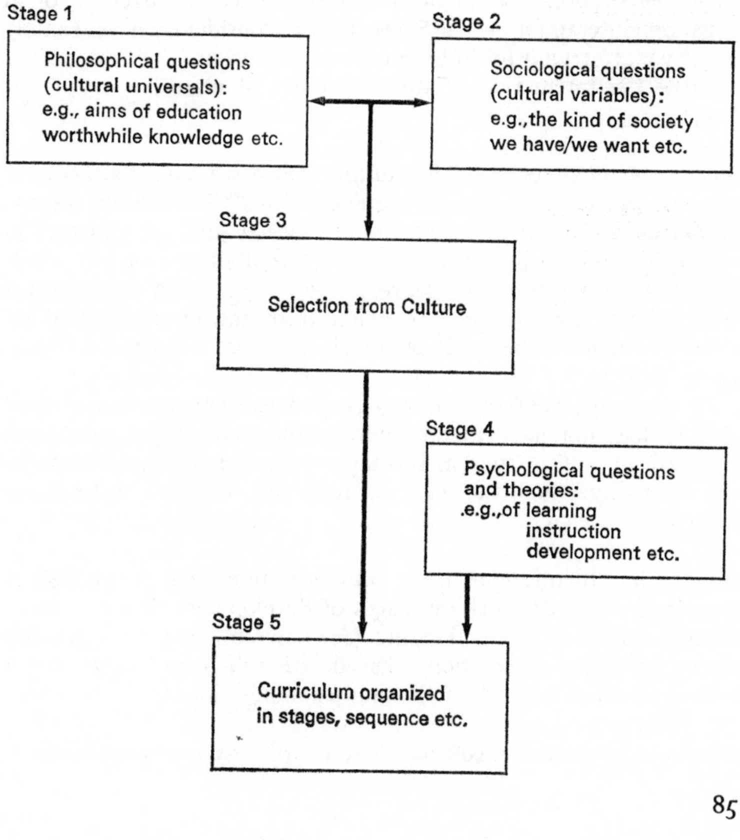

Stage 1: Philosophical questions All teachers have ideas about what they believe to be worthwhile or about the structure of knowledge, but most would benefit from re-thinking these ideas more systematically, considering their implications for practice, and seeing how these ideas interact with other kinds of questions, especially sociological issues.

Stage 2: Sociological questions (It might be argued that the order of Stages 1 and 2 should be reversed, i.e. that consideration of our society now, in practice, is likely to precede thinking about education in more general terms of cultural universals.)

This section will include complex questions about the kind of society we live in now; how and why it has developed in that way; the particular kinds of social change which are likely to be important in influencing education (technological changes, ideological changes, etc.). In practice, these kinds of question are rarely limited to a functional analysis of society as it has been and as it is now : almost inevitably we are drawn into considerations of how society *might be* or even *should be* improved. Hence the overlap, or at least the interaction with, Stage 1—the consideration of exactly what we are trying to do by means of education.

From the interaction of these two sets of questions we derive Stage 3.

Stage 3: A selection from the culture Once we have clarified, but not necessarily answered, such questions as 'What are our aims?', 'What do we mean by worthwhile?', 'What kind of pressures in society should we be influenced by?', 'What situations will pupils be faced with when they leave school?', etc., then we are in a better position to make a selection from the culture, based on criteria which can be made public even if total consensus is likely to be lacking.

At this stage the selection may be an ideal selection in the sense that it does not have to take into account either the limitations imposed by reality (such as shortage of teachers or equipment), or the means by which the selection from the culture is to be transmitted.

Stage 4 has therefore to bring into operation such psychological theories as Piaget's work on stages of development, Bruner's ideas about a theory of instruction, etc. (See Lawton, 1973, for a detailed discussion of this interaction.) Consideration of these factors would lead to the final stage of curriculum planning—Stage 5.

Stage 5: Curriculum organized in terms of stages, sequence etc.

Another result of considering the questions and theories of Stage 4 will be to prescribe certain kinds of teaching, and change the learning conditions in fairly radical ways. For example, it is most unlikely that there could be any psychological justification for the present practice of having a teacher/pupil ratio of 1:30 and lessons lasting forty minutes for *all* kinds of learning activity; but this is still the current practice in the majority of secondary schools. A pattern of organization based on flexible grouping is essential to achieve the kind of learning regarded as necessary in the preceding argument. It has sometimes been suggested that educational psychology tells us little about how to teach, but one important finding has been almost consistently ignored: namely that the size of a group of pupils and the structure of the group should be changed according to the kind of learning task. One of the interesting features of 'The Humanities Curriculum Project' (Stenhouse, 1973) is that the project team have insisted on half-classes arranged in a discussion circle—to attempt that kind of learning with groups of thirty pupils in rows facing the teacher would have been disastrous.

Given the kind of society we live in, and given a degree of acceptance of the kind of arguments I have outlined in Chapter 5 for a common culture curriculum based on publicly identifiable knowledge, we must now ask what such a curriculum might look like. I have already suggested that a common culture curriculum must be based on knowledge, and on disciplines, but with the caveat that knowledge should be interpreted widely and that there should be planned timetable provision for inter-disciplinary work. The school organization necessary to cope with this would be very different from the traditional subject-based structure. It will be an integrated curriculum in the sense that it will be carefully planned *as a whole*, not as a collection of disconnected 'subjects'.

Coverage and balance

From the point of view of society and from the point of view of the developing individual (in so far as these can be separated), we would want to offer a *general* education up to a reasonably high standard—an education which is not over-specialized, but covers as many forms of knowledge or realms of meaning as possible up to as high a standard as possible. This gives us the two important aspects of curriculum planning: *coverage* and *balance*. No important area should be missed out from our selection from the culture, but also the question of balance between the disciplines is very important.

I have already argued that one important task for curriculum planners is to reduce the complexity of the operation by thinking in terms of disciplines (or faculties) rather than subject departments. This is important for educational as well as organizational reasons. If we try to cope with 400 subjects, coverage and balance simply cannot operate; we certainly need to find a smaller number of manageable areas to work with and, as I argued in Chapter 5, knowledge divided into *disciplines* is a much more educationally respectable method of organization. But which of the many versions of the disciplines model should we operate with? How many disciplines? Even the limited number of theories reviewed in Chapter 5 differed in the number of disciplines to be included. How can schools make a rational choice? First, it may well be the case that some of the theorists put up better arguments for their system of classification than others—some schools may decide to base their curricular organization on Hirst, others on Phenix. But the second point I want to emphasize is that how a school decides to organize knowledge is *not* a purely philosophical question—there are important sociological and psychological factors as well. Some kind of regrouping of subject departments into disciplines is essential, for logical, psychological and administrative reasons, but there is no one pattern which will necessarily be best for all schools. I have elsewhere suggested (Lawton, 1969 and 1973) the following six core areas—five disciplines or faculties, and one inter-disciplinary unit —not necessarily taking up the same amount of time, but being regarded as essential ingredients or elements in every pupil's curriculum:

1. Mathematics.
2. The physical and biological sciences.
3. Humanities and social sciences (including history, geography, classical studies, social studies, literature, film and TV and religious studies).
4. The expressive and creative arts.
5. Moral education.
6. Inter-disciplinary work.

These would form five distinct disciplines or faculties, each with complete internal integration for the planning period—perhaps two, possibly even five years. They would be distinct, but not totally unrelated—clearly some of the five naturally touch upon each other more than others. For example, more contact and co-operation is necessary between mathematics and science than between mathematics and moral education. The inter-disciplinary element would be built in and planned as part of the whole curriculum.

An important principle emerges at this point: an essential feature of a common curriculum is that every pupil should reach a minimum level of understanding and experience in each of the five areas. Beyond that basic level, choice will be appropriate; in some areas the range of choice will be wider from the very beginning. For example, there may be more room for individual choice in the humanities than in mathematics; within the core of expressive and creative arts there may well be the greatest choice of all from the very beginning: everyone should know something about European studies but not everyone need learn to speak French and German. If we find that a pupil fails to achieve a basic understanding of science or mathematics, we must keep on trying but be prepared to change the *methods*—a different teacher, a different syllabus, programmed learning; the methods of teaching can and should be varied, but the ultimate goal should be preserved.

The theory behind this view of curriculum has emerged on previous pages: common schools are meaningless unless they transmit a common culture and provide an adequate means for individual development within the general framework of that culture. Without an insistence on a basic minimum understanding of the forms of knowledge which we regard as important, however, talk of equality of opportunity is no more than a sham and leads almost inevitably to non-academic courses for life-adjustment, i.e. the kinds of courses planned for 'less able' children, ostensibly, to prepare them for 'the world of work' and social relationships, but containing little or no worthwhile knowledge.

To operate this kind of integrated curriculum or common culture curriculum, a much greater degree of flexibility of organization will be necessary: team teaching may help, provided that it does not become a rigid and hierarchical device; flexible grouping of pupils will be an essential feature—I have already voiced my doubt about the one teacher and thirty pupils arrangement as the ideal learning group. To cater for individual interests and the wide range of abilities and previous achievements, the timetable will have to be thought of much more in terms of individual pupils than groups of thirty. The organization of such changes needs very careful planning, and teachers need also to re-think their attitudes and to re-examine their previous teaching-methods. This is perhaps the most difficult problem of all—the best plans will not succeed unless teachers are convinced and feel that the proposed changes are worthwhile.

This five- or six-fold division of the curriculum is based on the view that disciplines are important, but that as yet no complete picture of the disciplines has been firmly established. I have suggested a pattern based on five disciplines plus opportunities for planned inter-disciplinary work. It could be argued that seven or eight faculties would be better—for example, that humanities and social sciences should be separated. I would agree that a variety of patterns is not only possible but desirable at this stage, and some real variations will be considered in Chapter 7. My only plea would be that the divisions should not be arbitrary ones or matters of sheer expediency.

J. White: a compulsory curriculum?

My proposals for a common culture curriculum have much in common with John White's idea of a compulsory curriculum (*Towards a Compulsory Curriculum*, 1973). White's divisions of the compulsory curriculum are based on Hirst's forms of knowledge, but he takes the argument two stages further: he does not regard all the forms of knowledge as equally suitable as compulsory requirements, and he makes a major distinction between kinds of knowledge which have to be engaged in to produce understanding and those that do not. The resulting recommendation is an order of priorities: in the compulsory curriculum, humanities is logically prior to science, for example; and painting pictures, writing poetry and learning a foreign language become optional activities rather than compulsory requirements for all pupils. White's arguments are too complex for summary here, but I find his arguments for a rank-ordering of priorities very persuasive.

I should now like to consider some of the objections that may be raised to this kind of curriculum plan.

(a) That not all pupils are capable of benefiting from such a high-level common curriculum;
(b) that in practice it is not possible to organize a common curriculum for a wide range of pupil ability;
(c) that if such a curriculum plan is attempted it inevitably lowers standards and holds back bright pupils.

(a) That not all pupils are capable of benefiting from such a high-level common curriculum This is a commonly held assumption popular both with the general public and the teaching profession. It is a slightly different argument from Bantock's (see Chapter 2) since it is based on meritocratic rather than élitist assumptions. This view is connected with the 'fact' that many working-class pupils are of low intelligence, and teachers 'experience' that only intelligent pupils can do rigorous academic work. The view is based on assumptions with very little supporting empirical evidence. Only recently has the assumption even been questioned by educationists: for example, in Schools Council *Working Paper No. 2*:

The possibility of helping the pupils who are the concern of this Paper to enter the world of ideas, to use powers of reason, and to acquire even the beginnings of mature judgments, may seem to contradict the experience of many teachers. Indeed it may carry an almost revolutionary ring to some....

Psychological research has tended merely to accept the assumption and draw up methods of measuring failure by such question-begging devices as the 'normal curve'. Sociological research has been no more illuminating, tending to explain failure rather than to question the underlying assumptions.

I want to argue that the assumption that the majority of pupils are incapable of grasping the basic principles of the kind of common curriculum described above is a hangover from the nineteenth-century division into two kinds of education: élitist and elementary. Sociologists such as Turner (1964) have pointed out that education not only serves to promote social mobility but also to restrict it. Societies in the early, and even middle stages of industrialization have a supposed economic 'need' for only a small percentage of highly educated men. In such a situation one important function of 'schooling' (as opposed to education) is to restrict educational opportunity to the 'right' number. Thus schools in such societies are dominated by selection, streaming, competitive examinations and the problem of occupational placement.

There are two reasons why we should now look very critically at our own schooling system to see whether it resembles the above picture: first, it is a description of a school system rather than an educational system—by definition an educational system ought to promote individual abilities rather than to restrict them; second, a more mundane argument, which is that although we have left the phase of limited industrialization far behind, our schools are still concentrating on selecting and grading, and are now over-producing semi-skilled and unskilled workers; what we really need now—even in crude economic terms—is much more open access to higher levels of achievement.

In recent years the argument has tended to centre around the question of raising the school leaving age. Parents who pay fees in order to send their own children to independent schools (whatever their measured ability might be) often question the value of keeping others' children in state schools until sixteen. They seem not to question the capacity of their own children to profit from an academic education—even if they realize that their own children are not particularly able or intelligent—but they do question whether it is worth spending public money on the majority of children. The success of some public schools in coping adequately with less intellectual pupils is, however, important evidence on this question. There is also a growing amount of empirical evidence to suggest that teachers frequently underestimate the abilities of pupils—especially when the pupils come from working-class areas (Wilson, 1963; Halsey, 1972). There is certainly little support in the existing research to sustain the view that intelligence is the key factor in educational 'failure'—we must look to much more complex explanations in the direction of motivation, teachers' attitudes and curriculum.

(b) That in practice it is not possible to organize a common curriculum for a wide range of pupil ability The answer to this objection is that quite clearly it would be difficult or even impossible to organize it if we continued to try to operate with the old-fashioned grouping of one teacher instructing thirty pupils proceeding artificially in lock-step. A much more flexible arrangement is needed, clearly guided by principles of curriculum planning. A plan which would be appropriate for a humanities curriculum (but possibly not for a linear subject such as mathematics) would be the following:

Step 1 Make a selection of topics, or questions to be explored, and generalizations to be encouraged, which all pupils should be exposed to by the end of the period—perhaps a two- or three-year sequence. This selection should embody the basic *structure* of the discipline and the most important content to be covered.

Step 2 Arrange the topics in a *sequence*: for example, twelve topics, two for each term for a six-term period, in the best possible sequence of learning. Bruner has suggested that where sequence appears not to be important a kind of 'shuffle test' should be operated, and we should ask, if sequence does not appear to be important, have we missed any opportunities.

Step 3 For each basic core-topic, work out additional topics or themes at a variety of levels of difficulty and also catering for a variety of individual interests. Thus some pupils will spend most (but not all) of their time on the basic topics whilst others will be reaching considerably greater levels of depth in that particular area. It should not, however, be assumed that those who cover most ground are necessarily the ablest. Some children work quickly but superficially. It is an important aspect of the teacher's role in this to ensure that sufficient basic learning is taking place.

In diagrammatic form, the three steps may be envisaged as follows:

Step 1 Selection of topics 1-12 for one year's work. Main concerns: selection of material to convey the overall structure of the discipline; understanding general principles and important content; what the discipline or subject is all about.

Step 2 *Sequence:* conversion of topics 1-12 into a pattern of development A-L.

Term 1	Term 2	Term 3
A—B—C—D		
	—E—F—G—H	
		—I—J—K—L

Main concern: *sequence,* to what extent is there a logical development of ideas and content?

Step 3 Catering for individual interests and abilities.

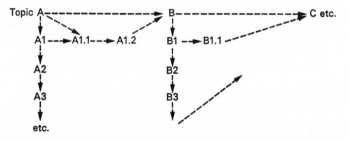

A pupil of modest ability might do little more than cover the basic work enshrined in topics A to L. But these basic topics will include the content and ideas thought to be essential common learning for all pupils. Other pupils will be able to go into greater depth (A1, A2, A3, etc.) before proceeding to topic B at the end of the period of, say, three weeks. Others may proceed from A to A1.1 and then to A1.2. In other words, an essential aspect of the common curriculum is that it must cater for a wide variety of interests and abilities. This is probably the most neglected aspect of curriculum planning in those schools operating with mixed-ability groups. The most common arrangement is for some pupils to be kept waiting while the majority of the class finish, which usually means that some pupils never finish anything to their own or to their teacher's satisfaction. Preparing several additional 'depth' and 'breadth' topics as well as the basic topics does mean an enormous amount of preparatory work for teachers—but it is essential if the common culture curriculum is to work adequately. Unfortunately,

93

publishers have not yet shown themselves to be particularly helpful in this respect. The task is not as great as might appear at first sight, however. For example, topic A3 might well be to read a book and write an essay afterwards; or topic A1.1 might be to look at a filmstrip and answer a few questions on it. Not all the teaching materials required have to be created by the teachers; it is sometimes much better to use and adapt existing materials. If this is done, there is no reason at all why the organization of a mixed-ability group should present insuperable difficulties.

(c) If such a curriculum plan is attempted it inevitably lowers standards and holds back bright pupils This is the point of view of those educationalists who tend to see comprehensive education as a 'threat to standards' or as a dangerous 'progressive' innovation likely to destroy the traditional means of selecting and grooming future leaders. Many variations of such objections can be found in some of the contributions to the first *Black Paper* (edited by Cox and Dyson, 1969). In some unstreamed situations, where teachers try to carry on traditional methods of teaching, it is almost certainly true that standards fall and bright pupils may be held back. But it has also been argued (Goldberg and Passow, 1966) that streaming holds back the very bright pupils because they are treated simply as A pupils when they may well be A + + in that particular kind of learning. The advantage of the common-culture, individualized curriculum described in this chapter is that all pupils can be allowed to work at their own pace and encouraged to go forward as fast and as far as they possibly can. This is certainly not true of the typical A-stream arrangement in most schools. In this context it may be worthwhile referring to the 'Plowden Report' (1967) which had doubts about streaming, not because the members felt that all children were the same but because they were *so* different.

Potentially, then, the individualized common curriculum is a means of improving standards, not lowering them. This will apply to the whole range of ability including the ablest as well as the lowest 25 per cent who, according to Keith Gardner (1968), at present leave school insufficiently adept at reading to cope adequately with a daily newspaper. Clearly, the present system of roughly classifying pupils as A, B, C, etc., has very serious limitations. But the problem goes much deeper than that: embedded in the thinking of a large number of teachers is the expectation of failure. This is the direct result of working within a school system which, I have suggested above, is based on selecting and grading, and where the dominant metaphor is a race with winners and losers. The solution to this problem is thus not simply a question of curriculum development by producing the appropriate materials, as suggested in (b) above; it is also a question of changing teachers' attitudes. There is no curriculum development possible without teacher development.

Benjamin Bloom has described a similar, but not identical problem in the USA in an important paper 'Mastery Learning and its Implications for Curriculum Development' (in Eisner, 1971, p. 17):

Each teacher begins a new term—or course—with the expectation that about a third of his students will adequately learn what he has to teach. He expects about a third of his students to fail or just get by. Finally, he expects another third to learn a good deal of what he has to teach, but not enough to be regarded as good students. This set of expectations supported by school policies and practices in grading, becomes transmitted to the students through the grading procedures and through the methods and materials of instruction. This system creates a self-fulfilling prophecy such that the final sorting of students through the grading process becomes approximately equivalent to the original expectations. This set of expectations, which fixes the academic goals of teaching and students, is the most wasteful and destructive aspect of the present educational system. It reduces the aspirations of both teachers and students, it reduces motivation for learning in students, and it systematically destroys the ego and self concept of a sizeable group of the students who are legally required to attend school....

Bloom suggests that most students—perhaps more than 90 per cent are capable of *mastering* what we want to teach them. But to achieve this kind of 'mastery learning' a quite different attitude to curriculum and teaching is needed—above all by the teachers. When it comes to evaluation, teachers are obsessed with the 'normal curve' by means of which a small number are expected to perform well, the majority are expected to be mediocre, and some *must* fail. But the normal curve is best suited to chance or random activities, whereas education is supposed to be a purposeful activity—and the purpose should now be to achieve a satisfactory amount of progress for *all* pupils.

Bloom does not dispute that pupils have different aptitudes for various subjects but we have to ask whether low aptitude simply excuses a teacher for failing to teach. Bloom accepts Carroll's (1963) view that 'aptitude is the amount of time required by the learner to attain mastery of a learning task'. The educational disease diagnosed by Carroll in his 'A model of school learning' (1963) is precisely that despite differences in aptitude, the usual practice in schools is to provide all pupils with roughly the same kind of instruction and the same amount of instruction. The solution is clear: for pupils with lower aptitude in a specific area of the curriculum *more* time should be spent, but not simply more of the same kind of instruction—different approaches and teaching techniques will be essential to prevent boredom and rebellion. In this respect we have as yet hardly begun to make use of available techniques. As Taylor points out (1971), a medical Rip Van Winkle would be completely lost in a modern operating theatre, but a teacher from the nineteenth century would feel quite at home between the rows of desks and the blackboards.

Bloom and Carroll both argue that given a good tutor (and enough time) nearly every pupil could achieve a high degree of success in any subject. Bloom (1971) quotes unpublished research by Dave (1963) to show that for some pupils on a mathematics course the correlation between low mathematical aptitude and the end-of-year examination results was zero. For these mainly middle-class pupils their poor ability was adequately compensated for by the fact that they received just as much individual tutoring in mathematics at home as they had group instruction in the classroom. By contrast, for those who received no help outside the classroom, the correlation between aptitude and achievement was 0·9. The claim is now forcefully being made in the USA that low aptitudes *can* be compensated by more time and more appropriate instruction. It would, of course, be naïve and dangerous to assume that more time alone would produce the desired results—the International Study of Achievement in Mathematics (Husen, 1967) showed a low correlation between time spent and achievement. The key variable seems to be willingness to *persist*, which in turn is related to the appropriateness of the instruction rather than the simple amount of time spent. The satisfaction of short-term successes by the pupils is very important. A further discussion of these views may be found in Chapter 3 of Bloom *et al.*, (1971).

One doubt which some British teachers may have about the approach adopted in the *Handbook on Formative and Summative Evaluation of Student Learning* (Bloom *et al.*, 1971) is its close connection with the objective approach to curriculum planning. There is no reason, however, why the Bloom and Carroll view of mastery-learning should not be applied to a much more flexible curriculum plan such as I have outlined above. It is necessary in any curriculum to have clear ideas about what should be aimed at, but this does not mean that everything has to be translated into sets of behavioural objectives. Cronbach makes this point very clearly in his comments on Bloom's proposals for mastery learning (in Eisner, 1971, p. 53):

Bloom makes a number of statements implying a closed model

of instruction. We have to get the pupil to master what the teacher has to teach, he says—but the teacher has it in his power to teach *more* than he, the teacher, knows. The pupil has to be equipped to deal with the world the teacher has not lived in. To stipulate that the teacher has a limited set of formulas to pass on is to retreat from the problems of instruction that perplex and interest me. I see educational development as continuous and open-ended. Mastery seems to imply that at some point we get to the end of what ought to be taught.

The most important message from Bloom, however, is that schools must have a variety of instructional devices available: programmed instruction may help some pupils; work-sheets or work-books may suit others; audio-visual methods and games are still very rarely used; groups of pupils working together in co-operation rather than competition have been found to be an effective way of improving some kinds of learning.

Another principle that follows from this is the need for the content of the curriculum to be looked at very carefully. If we are going to expect all pupils to learn something then we ought to be able to justify its inclusion in the curriculum—not only to ourselves but to the pupils. If pupils are compelled to attend schools, teachers have a moral duty not to waste their time and to trivialize the educational process. In order to achieve this, teachers must all become experts in curriculum planning. This may seem a tall order but in a decentralized system such as ours, there would appear to be no alternative.

Summary

In this chapter, I have attempted to outline the processes by which teachers might plan a common culture curriculum. It is always important to emphasize that a common curriculum does not imply holding pupils down to a minimum level of achievement or even to a minimum content. One aspect of a common curriculum is that it sets out the main areas or disciplines to be experienced by all pupils, and also the main features of those disciplines to be covered by all. But beyond these basic minima all pupils should be encouraged to delve deeper and wider. Thus an appropriate description of such a curriculum might be a common-culture, individualized curriculum. To cope with individual interests and abilities, I have emphasized the need for a wide variety of methods and materials to be made available for the basic topics and also for the additional depth and breadth topics. Where this kind of careful preparation and planning takes place, criticisms of mixed-ability teaching do not hold; but in addition to curriculum materials being available, for this kind of curriculum to work, we also need to have teachers whose attitudes to pupils' learning do not impose unnecessary limitations on their levels of achievement. The three most important factors in this reformed educational process are: a worthwhile and relevant curriculum; the availability of carefully planned materials and methods suited to a wide range of abilities and interests; and perhaps most important of all, teachers who believe that this kind of curriculum for all pupils is desirable and possible.

The next chapter will discuss some schools where common curricula are being implemented.

7

Common culture curricula
in three schools

In this chapter, I want to look at three very different secondary schools all of which have planned the curriculum on the basis of mixed-ability groupings of pupils and a basic common core curriculum for all pupils. None of the schools would wish, of course, to restrict or limit their pupils' achievement to some kind of lowest common denominator. They see the essence of a common culture curriculum as one which stipulates a basic minimum curriculum that *should* be covered, but never the maximum that could be covered—it is completely open-ended for individuals.

Sheredes School is a school which started off with considerable advantages: a new, purpose-built school, a young staff specially selected to create a new kind of curriculum and teaching-style, a head whose experience combined practical work in comprehensive schools with theoretical studies of curriculum planning. Some would also include among the advantages of the school the fact that its catchment area, although very mixed, does not generally include the kind of 'multi-deprivation' that Thomas Calton School has to cope with.

Thomas Calton School, on the other hand, has been chosen as an example of a school which can plan a rigorous, demanding curriculum despite its considerable disadvantages and problems. Its buildings are old and often unsuited to any kind of learning other than formal classwork; the head took it over as a 'going concern' four years ago—at a time when staff and pupils' morale was low. In some respects it is still at a transitional stage of curriculum development; its first three years are in completely mixed ability groups, but years four and five, although much more 'open' than most schools, segregate—to some limited extent—the pupils into three groups: the 'O' level, the CSE and the non-examination pupils. Whereas Sheredes can get away with treating all its pupils as potential CSE candidates at least, the ability range of Thomas Calton is such that this would be very difficult at present. Thus a certain amount of separation is forced on the school by the examination structure. They have temporarily compromised without sacrificing the benefits of mixed-ability groups in the earlier years. It is pragmatic, where Sheredes is grounded in theory—but the outcome in terms of curriculum content does not appear to be very different.

Finally, Chatham South School is at an interesting planning stage. It started with a skeleton staff of teachers since there were only 120 pupils (first year) in the school. These teachers had to cover the whole curriculum between them, so the head made a virtue out of necessity by creating what is in effect a faculty structure very similar in some respects to that of Sheredes School. The basic core of eight 'areas' is maintained until the fourth year, when greater diversification takes place—but this is specialization based on the foundation, basic work of the first three years.

The following descriptions of the curricula of the three schools were written for a conference at the University of London Institute of Education in 1973 by the three headmasters who have kindly given permission for the reports to be reproduced here.

Sheredes School

Curriculum and organization The curriculum is based on the view that a liberal education can, and should, be offered to all pupils in a comprehensive school during their compulsory five years' schooling. Sheredes School opened as a purpose-built five-form entry all-ability school in the Hertfordshire reorganisation scheme in 1969 with first-year pupils only but with complete 11-18 school buildings with sixth form provision included. These pupils are now (1973) in their fifth year and take 16-plus examinations next summer. There are at present 712 in all on roll.

The aim of the core curriculum is to initiate pupils into those forms of knowledge and understanding which, following recent work by philosophers of education, might be supposed to form the basic equipment of an educated person. On this view, the school's chief task is to transmit the culture by way of a general education concerned with the development of mind in differentiated modes of consciousness and experience. The areas that may be distinguished include mathematics, the physical sciences, moral awareness, aesthetic experience, religious concepts, and an awareness and understanding of our own and other people's minds. In some cases these can be directly related to existing subjects, but in others the areas must be covered, as in a jigsaw, by interrelations between existing subjects. For a problem may call for different sorts of enquiry; and it is not always most appropriate to present the differing disciplines in their worked-out forms.

Another implication is that, since the needs of the whole range of ability must be met, the format must enable staff to develop a variety of learning patterns, certainly with scope for individual and group work; and staff will need access to a resource facility if suitable materials are to be generated and made available. A longer unit of time than the usual 35-minute lesson will be generally advantageous, and by working in teams staff will be able to provide the necessary variety of approaches and experiences. And given that these exist, logic suggests they should be made available to all pupils, so that the organisation of learning matches the child's changing response.

These are all pointers in the direction of a faculty structure with an unstreamed format, and Table 1 illustrates the arrangement for the first five years. In addition to the core curriculum, provision must be made to meet certain further instrumental and vocational requirements and the options indicated allow for this. The 3rd year option A offers all pupils access to an introductory course in a second language, while in the 4th and 5th years options B and C meet this and other specialist needs. This option time is only 20 per cent of the 4th/5th year curriculum, and the scheme is thus roughly the reverse of that common in most comprehensive schools. The point is that the core curriculum offers a measure of intrinsic choice within faculties to meet pupils' varying abilities and interests.

Pastoral organisation is based on a year-tutor system with no lower/upper school division. But the School Forum arrangements take account of varying needs with age, and each Forum meets and reports back weekly in school time. School reports are sent annually, drawing particularly on the termly assessments of pupils' progress made by staff in each faculty. There is a flourishing parent-teacher association.

TABLE I   *Curriculum Structure: Sheredes School*

	Faculties	Year	Subjects	Examinations 16+
Common core	Humanities[1]	1,2,3,4,5, →	English,History, Geography	3 (mode 3)
	Expressive arts →		English,Music, Drama	0 (or 1 Music for some who opt)[2]
	Mathematics →		Mathematics	1
	Creative activities →		Art, Handicraft, Housecraft	1 (Design)[3]
	Physical activities →		P.E.,Games	0
	Science[4] →		Schools Council Integrated Science	1
	Languages →		French	0
Options	A[6]			
	B		Science[5],Tech.Drawing, French,Art,Woodwork, Typing,Office Practice, Auto English	1
	C		Science[5] Latin, Commerce, Metalwork, German, Cookery, Office Practice, Typing	1

Notes

1. Humanities course also includes moral and religious education.
2. Music O-level only an adjunct and involves some after-school time.
3. An interrelated course linking Art and Handicraft and including Housecraft.
4. One pass in Integrated Science (SCISP, GCE or Mode 3 CSE).
5. Offers second SCISP, GCE pass, also Human Biology and Physics with Chemistry.
6. Option A (3rd year) subjects: Latin, German (introductory courses), Science, Wood, Metal, Housecraft, Art/English linked course.

Organisation Summary

1. 20 periods weekly, each 70 minutes: 2 in the morning, 2 in the afternoon.
2. Allocation includes double period weekly for Humanities and Creative Arts.
3. Following are taught, whole year group at a time, with

minimum of 6 staff: Humanities, Creative Arts (part of physical activities). Remainder taught in half-year groups. Thus time-table is consistently blocked out by faculties.

4. Year-tutor (horizontal) system for pastoral care: 150 pupils with five form tutors. Each pupil placed in one of five unstreamed forms and in one of six subject groups to facilitate faculty organisation (all total mixed ability).

5. Boys and girls from each form elected termly to appropriate Forum (three for whole of school), meeting weekly and reporting back to forms.

Sixth Form   The curriculum pattern after the first five years was the subject of a residential staff conference. Three guiding principles were generally agreed. First, the 'common-core' concept behind years 1 to 5 should be carried forward as sixth form central studies, a mandatory 4 periods weekly (out of 20, as before) which would take a central theme like 'limits to growth' and exploit it in terms of different forms of understanding—represented by a team of teachers assembled for each of the 4 periods—for a given unit of course time. This would be a coherent programme, rather than the option-based general studies programmes usually offered, and one that ought to help energise related Advanced Level studies and other courses. Secondly, one period of allocated time for each examination subject would be flexibly available, for use either formally or for seminar or tutorial work. Finally, it was recognised that the introduction of a coherent, compulsory central studies component should offer both breadth and balance and thus leave sixth-formers free to choose examination subjects on a totally free basis, limited only by timetabling or career considerations. This would seem to be a sounder solution both logically and psychologically, than the recent School Council proposals for providing a broader course, and can be introduced without changing the existing exam structure. But there would be no difficulty about making use of the Certificate of Extended Education in our scheme in principle, and we shall do so to an extent determined by the curriculum content and acceptability of CEE courses. Our scheme can also be adapted to suit the 'N' and 'F' proposals if these ultimately are implemented.

M. HOLT
Headmaster

Thomas Calton School

Curriculum and Organisation   Thomas Calton is a mixed, 7 form

entry (1000 boys and girls) Comprehensive School in a deprived
area of South East London. The school operates in two ancient
buildings, nearly 100 years old, separated by half a mile. The
Lower School comprises years 1, 2 and 3; the Upper School, years
4, 5 and 6. We have four 'outposts'—a woodwork shop in the
playground of a local primary school, a domestic science unit
in yet another primary school, a detached ROSLA complex and
half a week's use of another workshop.

Our curriculum is geared to the eventual building of a new
school—designed for integration, team teaching, flexibility and
community involvement. Within the constraints imposed by our
present physical environment we are attempting to evolve both
an integrated curriculum and team teaching.

Our intake is heavily loaded towards the less academic range:
we have many children who suffer from multi-deprivation.
Therefore there is a strong emphasis upon strengthening our social
welfare work as part of a process of 'compensation'. This in turn,
leads to attempts to stimulate interest, raise motivational and
expectation levels and give our youngsters a chance to become
mature, young adults, equipped with the necessary skills and
awareness to cope with life.

We put a heavy weighting on remedial work and boosting reading
in the Lower School. As part of this we run a Summer Holiday
'Headstart Project' for some 40 of our September intake in the
weeks immediately preceding their official arrival here. This is
a mixed course of activities, trips and visits, with a team of
teachers and students with children selected because they are
under-achievers or have emotional problems.

In Years 1 and 2 there is no streaming [See Table 2]. For half the
week each year is timetabled (whole mornings and afternoons)
for Integrated Studies. Their form teacher is their class teacher,
and the year team is supplemented by specialist Art, Music,
Foreign Language, Remedial and Drama teachers. The work is
thematic e.g. this term Year 1's topic is 'Ourselves'. Integrated
Studies includes English, History, Geography, Social Studies, R.E.,
Art, Music, Drama, Remedial work and small group French or
German. Science, Maths, P.E. and Games are taught separately
and there is also a form period. Woodwork, Needlework, Cookery
and extra Art are given on a 'rotating group' basis.

TABLE 2

Structure	30 period week		
Year 1	16 periods		I.S.
	5	,,	P.E. and Games
	2	,,	Science
	4	,,	Maths
	2	,,	Handicrafts/Cookery etc.
	1	,,	Music
Year 2	14	,,	I.S.
	5	,,	P.E. and Games
	3	,,	Science
	4	,,	Maths
	2	,,	Handicrafts/Cookery
	1	,,	Music
	1	,,	Form period
Year 3	4	,,	English
	4	,,	Maths
	3	,,	History
	3	,,	Geography
	4	,,	Science
	3	,,	P.E. & Games
	1	,,	Social Studies
	2	,,	T.D./Needlework
	2	,,	Metalwork/Cookery
	2	,,	Art
	2	,,	French/extra English
Years 4 & 5	5	,,	English
	5	,,	Maths
	4	,,	Community Education, Social Studies
	2	,,	Games/Activities
	4	,,	Option A
	4	,,	Option B
	4	,,	Option C
	2	,,	Option D

In Year 3 we give the full range of specialist subjects, but attempt to co-operate between English, History and Geography. In Games we open up choice, including Dance/Drama. There is no streaming. French or German is taught to those who show an interest and/or aptitude. The reason for the cross the board

Option A	Option B	Option C	Option D
History	History	German	Additional
Geography	Geography	French	English
Chemistry	Biology	Biology	Additional
Physics	Art	Physics	Maths
Catering	T.D.	Art	Computer
Needlework	Metalwork	T.D.	Studies
(Tailoring)	Child Develop-	Home	Building Studies
Metalwork	ment	Economics	Photography
Woodwork	Home	Metalwork	Dance/Drama
	Economics	Needlework	Design
			Music

> Year 6   CSE courses in most subjects
> 'O' level courses in most subjects
> 'A' level courses in 12 subjects
> Also a Business Studies course

subject experience is to give youngsters the chance to become aware of specialist disciplines to evaluate them to make judgment based choices for their 4th and 5th year courses.

In Years 4 and 5 everyone does English and Maths—these are block-timetabled so that all Year 4 English is at the same time— and so too for Maths. There are four option groups of subjects, three of which are exam orientated (we run our own CSE Mode 3 English). The fourth option column is non-exam. All Fourth Years spend a complete morning each week with a team of teachers in a Community Education Course, involving short 6 week courses in Social Studies, Careers, Race Relations, Ethics and at least a term of community service, working in local pre-school play-groups, nursery and infants' classes, old people's homes etc.

The pattern is repeated in Year 5, except that the Social Studies becomes more formalised.

The whole of the Upper School (Years 4, 5 and 6) combine for a Games/Activities afternoon, when a choice of 20 possibilities are on offer, ranging from horse-riding, skating and squash to design technology, chess, electronics and drama.

In the Upper School we run an Extended Day, a third session, offering nearly 30 different courses and activities.

The 6th Form timetable is much geared to individual needs and gives a mixture of CSE, 'O' level and 'A' level courses. We also have links with local colleges of Further Education. We are working towards establishing at least four periods a week of a 'Common Core' course.

RON PEPPER
Headmaster

Chatham South School

Curriculum and Organisation   Chatham South Secondary School is a new four-form entry Secondary Modern school which opened in September 1973 with a first-year intake of 120 boys and girls. There are plans to reorganise schools on comprehensive lines in the Medway area and it is therefore important that the initial organisation and curriculum is of such a nature that changes in the future should not prove too disruptive.

Organisation of the Curriculum   Because the school is organised internally into mixed-ability groups of children, there is a natural movement towards more flexible teaching methods in general and towards an increase in resource-based learning in particular. The aim is that every pupil should reach a minimum level of under-standing and experience in each area of the curriculum and that, beyond this minimum level, choice is both appropriate and desirable. Each child should, therefore, have the opportunity of studying a subject, of applying the knowledge so gained, and of combining it with other subjects in a practical and interesting way.
    The curriculum has been divided into the following areas of study:

1. Basic Subjects—English and Mathematics.
2. Science—including Physics, Chemistry, Biology and Rural Science.
3. Humanities—historical, geographical, social, religious and moral aspects.
4. Modern Languages—the language and culture of at least one other country.
5. Physical and recreational activities—P.E., dance, drama, movement, music.
6. Home Economics—the domestic sciences.
7. Arts and crafts—including woodwork, metalwork, art, pottery technical drawing.

Years 1, 2 and 3—a three-year basic course for all pupils (see Fig. 2).

Years 4 and 5—a two-year continuation course to cater for the needs of the individual pupils, bearing in mind their individual interests, differing abilities, requirements of external examinations and career prospects. There is a considerable direction to ensure that each child follows a broad-based course but, thereafter, self-selection is the over-riding principle.

The details of the core curriculum together with the options are best seen in Figure 2.

Each child must take:

(1) Further work in the basic subjects—English and Mathematics.
(2) Recreational activities—(non-examinable).
(3) A general course involving social education, moral education and personal relationships—(non-examinable).
(4) At least one option but not more than three options from:
   (a) Science;
   (b) Humanities;
   (c) Art, Craft and Home Economics.
   N.B. if *only one* option is taken from (a), (b) or (c), it must be the general course within that area.

General Information   The pastoral care is based on a form-tutor/Year Head system.

Considerable importance is attached to home/school communication and understanding.

All subjects are at present taught to class units, but pupils have opportunities to work individually and in groups.

There are 24 periods per week each of one hour duration.

D. SMYTH
Headmaster

Discussion

I would like to emphasize that this discussion of the three schools' curricula is in no sense an evaluation. I have merely selected three schools, known to me personally, as examples of different approaches and stages in development of common curricula. All three schools are committed to notions of social justice in education which give rise to a desire to educate young people of all abilities together, and also to a conviction that in order to achieve this ideal a planned common curriculum is essential. Beyond that basic similarity, significant differences begin to emerge.

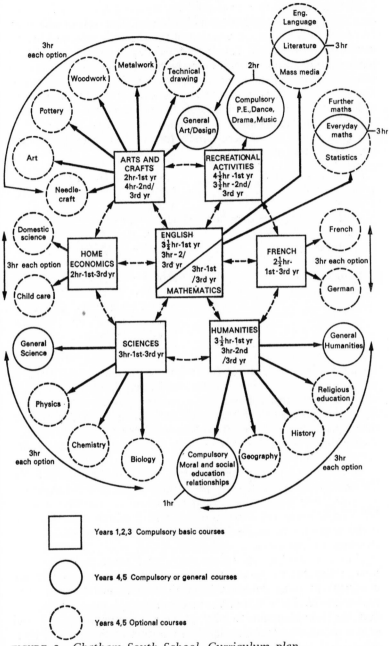

FIGURE 2   *Chatham South School, Curriculum plan*

109

Sheredes School, for example, has a curriculum clearly based on a theory of knowledge derived from Hirst. The view of education behind the curriculum plan is that of the generally educated person in the liberal tradition. This is reflected in the idea of all children having the opportunity (and even the necessity at the early stages) of experiencing *all* the forms of knowledge. The curriculum is not, however, a slavish imitation of Hirst's seven forms of knowledge: as I suggested in Chapter 6, schools have to pay heed to social and psychological factors as well as philosophical. It is interesting in this connection to compare Hirst's forms of knowledge with the Sheredes faculty structure:

Hirst's Forms of Knowledge	*Sheredes Faculties*
1. Mathematics	1. Mathematics
2. Science	2. Science
3. Understanding our own and other people's minds	3. Humanities
	4. Expressive Arts
4. Aesthetic	5. Creative Activities
5. Moral	Moral education not separated into faculties but included in Humanities, Pastoral Care and the general work of school, e.g. Forum.
6. Religious	
7. Philosophical	
	6. Physical Activities
	7. Languages

One possible criticism of this might be that the social sciences are under-represented even in this curriculum, but the explanation might be that most children are expected to stay on to the sixth form or to proceed to Further Education where they could develop that aspect of knowledge. (It is also a possible criticism of the Hirst theory that it is difficult to see exactly where economics and political science belong.)

An interesting divergence from my proposals (Chapter 6) is the Sheredes creation of a Faculty for Modern and Classical Languages; according to my plan that would be part of a humanities course. but I have never yet come across a school which does this—the social pressures to maintain the high status of foreign language teaching are too great.

Thomas Calton School, on the other hand, seems to have a pragmatic rather than a theoretical approach. It might even be that the dominant thinking behind this curriculum is *social* rather than *philosophical*. There is a stress on community action and the part that the school ought to play in compensating for social and economic disadvantages. A significant feature of this curriculum is the central part played by Integrated Studies in the early years.

Some might want to question whether too much was being included in the programme of Integrated Studies and whether this is too great a responsibility for the co-ordinator of that course. Once again it is probable that the thinking behind this course is social (and perhaps psychological) rather than philosophical: in areas such as the Thomas Calton catchment area it is notoriously difficult to get children to adjust from the informal atmosphere of primary schools to the subject-based seven-teachers-a-day pattern typical of most secondary schools. (See Nisbet and Entwistle, 1969.)

Finally, Chatham South School. This is an example of an attempt to match a theoretical view of a core curriculum with the demands and limited staff of a new school. In some ways it is a more cautious plan than Sheredes—English as a 'subject' is retained, for example. In other respects it avoids the common dangers of an option system, i.e. that the core will effectively be lost in the name of freedom of choice. This curriculum preserves a careful balance between 'self-selection' and restraints imposed on freedom to choose: for example, the rule that if pupils (in 4th year) do not choose two science options they *must* choose general science. These are simple but effective methods of ensuring that genuine negotiation takes place between pupils and teachers without allowing pupils to opt out of essential elements of a balanced programme.

Finally, it might be interesting to compare what each school regards as the compulsory core (using the four areas of my own curriculum plan in so far as they apply) (see Table 3).

TABLE 3

	Sheredes Years	Thomas Calton Years	Chatham South Years
Mathematics	1-5	1-5	1-5
Science	1-5	1-3 (Option D has no science as such, in Years 4 & 5.)	1-5
Humanities	1-5	Integrated Studies for Years 1-2; Year 3 compulsory English, History, Geography, Social Studies; Years 4-5 *some* in all options.	1-5
Expressive Arts	1-5	1-5	1-5

I should like to stress again that this exercise should not be seen as an evaluation. In my view all three schools are developing in different but excellent ways. Perhaps the most interesting feature is that by this analysis Thomas Calton School has a 100 per cent common curriculum for Years 1-3 but after that some separation is found to be necessary. It remains to be seen whether, with the advantages of a new building in a few years time and the new facilities and accommodation more suitable for mixed-ability grouping, the completely common core will be extended to Years 4 and 5. On the other hand, it may well be the case that the staff will argue that after three years enough of the common curriculum has been covered on a compulsory basis and that it is then desirable for greater choice (i.e. options), at least in some areas, to take over. My own feeling is that more schools will move in the direction of retaining compulsory areas (or faculties) for the full five years but provide a great deal more variety and choice *within* them.

8

Summary and conclusion: social justice and education

This book is essentially about social justice in the provision of education in our society. Earlier in the century the argument about opportunity was focused on access to educational institutions (especially grammar schools and universities); it was assumed that if selection could be made 'fair' then the problem of educational opportunity would be solved. This assumption was wrong for at least two reasons. First, the problem of access was inevitably connected with the related problems of selection, achievement and performance, all of which are correlated with social class. Second, the assumption of fairness was based on a meritocratic view rather than one that was genuinely egalitarian. Today we have to ask whether it is any more 'just' that a person should be favoured and rewarded because he has a high IQ than because his father has a high income.

Thus the trend has been away from problems of selection to problems of school organization (such as comprehensive reorganization and streaming) and, more recently still, to questions of curriculum and access to knowledge: what is the point of common schools if they do not transmit common culture by means of a common curriculum?

But what do we mean by a common curriculum? I have argued that we should distinguish between a society which may to some extent be divided politically and economically from one which is divided in a more general, cultural sense. In other words I am arguing against a naïve and simplistic interpretation of the Marxian assumptions about the direct relationship of the economic substructure and the cultural superstructure. I would accept that in a capitalist society the interests of the capitalist class may be in conflict with those of workers, but that does not justify labelling all science, history, art, philosophy and morals as bourgeois.

There is enough in common between most members of our society to justify the term common culture and to justify our attempting to plan a common curriculum. Class and regional differences should not divert our attention away from knowledge as the basis of culture. The arguments for a common culture and a common curriculum are under attack from the Right and some parts of the Left. The attack from the Right is from those who are frankly élitist in their educational thinking. For them 'real' culture is high culture—essentially the preserve of a minority. To attempt to spread culture too widely by universal education will, according to this view, simply destroy it. A related point of view is that education is primarily concerned with educating future leaders. Such leaders need to be selected early and given the best possible education to equip them for their leadership roles.

Attacks on the common curriculum from the Left take at least two forms. There are those who want working-class children to have a working-class curriculum, and those who sometimes seem to want no curriculum at all. The first of these views rests on a mistaken assumption about knowledge (i.e. that knowledge can be divided into middle-class and working-class in some meaningful way). The second view—that of some free-school advocates—rests on such mistaken assumptions about children as that if left to themselves they would make an appropriate selection from the culture and devise their own curriculum.

In Chapter 3, I looked at the historical reasons for the development of different cultures or sub-cultures. The suffering and changes undergone by the working-class as a result of industrialization and political reaction in the eighteenth and nineteenth centuries have been underestimated. Thompson's explanations of the *making* of the working-class are particularly powerful and helpful in diagnosing social class differences, but these differences, although important, do not today allow us to identify a distinctively working-class culture. A heritage of knowledge and beliefs which includes mathematics, science, history, literature and, more recently, film and television is shared by all classes. Real differences in social class sub-cultures should not obscure this communality of heritage.

The light that Thompson throws on the class basis of our society has more relevance to the transmission of the curriculum than its content. There is nothing in Thompson's analysis of the English working-class that suggests their possession of alternative kinds of knowledge or their need for a radically different curriculum. Many of the characteristic distinctions between working-class and middle-class appear to be affective rather than cognitive —attitudes and values rather than knowledge. Such class differences may be very important, but they do not constitute the basis for a totally different kind of curriculum.

In Chapter 4, I examined the same question from the point of view of the sociology of knowledge. We need to separate political–economic differences and conflicts in society from questions about its cognitive and cultural basis. Our sympathy with some of the views expressed by certain sociologists about the unfair distribution of educational knowledge must not obscure much more difficult questions about knowledge as a basis of curriculum planning. The debate about the social distribution of knowledge and the stratification of knowledge is important: equality of educational opportunity certainly should imply equality of access to knowledge. But some sociologists of knowledge go much further and question the validity of knowledge itself, suggesting that all knowledge is socially constructed and therefore relative, i.e. that one man's view of reality or knowledge is as good as another's. In one sense, to say that knowledge is socially constructed is merely stating the obvious: if knowledge is shared by a number of people it must be social. It does not follow, however, that all interpretations of reality are equally valid. Sociologists of knowledge such as Marx, Mannheim and others, eventually find themselves in the paradoxical position of claiming that all knowledge is merely the product of particular social situations—except their own views. My main argument is that certain interpretations of reality can be seen to be much less 'distorted' than others. It is these kinds of knowledge that should be the basis of curriculum planning.

I went on to argue, in Chapter 5, that if knowledge is the basis of curriculum planning, then it makes sense to divide knowledge into manageable areas by means of the academic disciplines with which we are familiar. What we actually call disciplines may be less important than making use of the distinctive concepts, structures, and truth tests which are firmly established as aspects of our intellectual heritage. Whether these are intrinsic to the structure of knowledge or 'man-made' is an interesting issue but not the central one as far as curriculum planning is concerned. If we are to transmit knowledge to the next generation then there are clear advantages in transmitting it in structured forms. This does *not* mean, however, that I want to present an apologia for the traditional grammar school curriculum, *nor* does it mean that a common culture based firmly on disciplines would not involve various kinds of integration or inter-disciplinary work. One of the valid criticisms of the traditional secondary curriculum is that it has not succeeded in relating disciplines to each other nor to the real world outside schools. The traditional secondary curriculum is also sadly lacking in both adequate coverage of knowledge areas and a balance between them.

In Chapter 6, I set out some suggestions for planning a common curriculum which would combine the kinds of knowledge with which everyone in our society needs to have some familiarity, and the possibility of all pupils pursuing their own interests to an optimum extent. It is important to emphasize that the common curriculum is not a device for bringing everyone down to the same level; it is a means of opening up knowledge and experience for all pupils whatever their ability might be. Thus it is not only a common curriculum but a common culture curriculum which is individualized rather than made uniform. Some of the objections to such a curriculum disappear when the quality of the content of the curriculum is matched with equally good materials and teaching-methods suitable for mixed-ability groups. Having a range of materials and methods available to transmit the common curriculum is difficult and expensive, but essential. The three necessary ingredients for a successful development of this kind are: curriculum content which is both worthwhile and meaningful to the pupils; appropriately selected methods and materials for a range of abilities; and finally, teachers with appropriate attitudes and skills.

In Chapter 7, I have included three examples of schools which are attempting to put a common curriculum into practice. They are very different from one another and the curriculum patterns outlined reflect these differences. There is no one magic formula which will suit all comprehensive schools in the country. Nevertheless there are certain general principles which apply. In this book, I have concentrated on a common culture and a common curriculum, but this does not mean that individual differences do not matter. It is unfortunate that in some educational debates 'the individual' is opposed to 'society'. Part of the purpose of this book has been to stress the inter-dependence of the two: we only become truly human and individual by interacting with other people and by participating in the general culture of that society. An important feature of education is to promote that aspect of culture known as knowledge.

To achieve a completely just society would involve changes outside as well as inside education. In this book I have not been concerned with general inequalities nor with such questions as parental choice and fee-paying schools; my discussion has focused simply on the curriculum as one aspect of the fairness or justice of treating people similarly or differently in education. According to ideas about distributive justice which have been discussed by Rawls (1972) and others, it would seem to follow that pupils should have access to the same kind of curriculum unless good reasons can be shown for providing different curricula: the onus is on those who wish to provide different curricula, to demonstrate that this will be 'fair'. I have suggested that social class differences do not provide sufficient reasons for stipulating different kinds of curricula; for reasons of interest and particular abilities some pupils will certainly go further in some directions than others. But the basic provision—the common curriculum—should be organized so that it is open to everyone. Anything less than this for normal pupils will not be socially just.

Suggestions for further reading

For a more detailed discussion of the historical background to the present curricular problems, I would suggest some of the other volumes in the Students Library of Education series: for example, Eaglesham, *The Foundations of Twentieth-Century Education*, Rubinstein and Simon, *The Evolution of the Comprehensive School 1926-1972*, and Bernbaum, *Social Change and the Schools: 1918-1944*. Parkinson, *The Labour Party and the Organization of Secondary Education 1918-1965* is also very useful

On the question of culture and education Williams, *Culture and Society 1780-1950* (Pelican, 1963) and *The Long Revolution* (Pelican, 1961) are essential reading; and Stenhouse, *Culture and Education* (Nelson, 1967) relates the general discussion to classroom practice. Hirst and Peters, *The Logic of Education* (Routledge & Kegan Paul, 1970) also relate these questions to the content of the curriculum. Altick, *The English Common Reader* (Chicago U.P., 1957) discusses the question of class and education in a very readable way. Julia Evetts, *The Sociology of Educational Ideas* (Routledge & Kegan Paul, 1973) provides an interesting introduction to some of the newer approaches to the sociology of education—including sociology of knowledge.

John White, *Towards a Compulsory Curriculum* (Routledge & Kegan Paul, 1973) provides us with a new approach to an unusual topic in English education. For further discussion of the common curriculum see Lawton, *Social Change, Educational Theory and Curriculum Planning* (ULP, 1973).

Bibliography

ALTICK, R. D. (1957), *The English Common Reader: A History of the Mass Reading Public 1800-1900*, Chicago University Press.

ARGYRIS, C. (1964), *Personality and Organisation*, Harper and Row.

ARMYTAGE, W. H. G. (1964), *Four Hundred Years of English Education*, Cambridge University Press.

AUSUBEL, D. P. (1959), 'Human growth and development', reprinted in De Cecco, J. P. (ed.) (1963), *Human Learning in the School*, Holt, Rinehart & Winston.

BANKS, O. (1955), *Parity and Prestige in English Secondary Education*, Routledge & Kegan Paul.

BANTOCK, G. H. (1968), *Culture, Industrialisation and Education*, Routledge & Kegan Paul.

BANTOCK, G. H. (1971), 'Towards a theory of popular education', in Hooper, R. (1971).

BARNES, D. (ed.) (1969), *Language, the Learner and the School*, Penguin.

BELSON, W. A. (1967), *The Impact of Television*, Crosby Lockwood.

BENEDICT, R. (1934), *Patterns of Culture*, various editions.

BENGE, R. C. (1970), *Libraries and Cultural Change*, Clive Bingley.

BENN, C., and SIMON, B. (1970), *Half Way There*, McGraw-Hill.

BERGER, P., and LUCKMAN, T. (1966), *The Social Construction of Reality*, Allen Lane.

BERNSTEIN, B. B. (1967), 'Open schools, open society', *New Society*, 14 September.

BERNSTEIN, B. B. (1970), 'A critique of the concept compensatory education', in Rubinstein, D., and Stoneman, C. (eds), *Education for Democracy*, Penguin.

BLOOM, B. S. (1971), 'Mastery learning and its implications for curriculum development', in Eisner (1971).

BLOOM, B. S., HASTINGS, J. T., and MADAUS, F. (1971), *Handbook of Formative and Summative Evaluation of Student Learning*, McGraw-Hill.

BRIGGS, A. (1967), 'The language of "class" in early nineteenth-century England', in Briggs and Saville (1967).

BRIGGS, A., and SAVILLE, J. (eds) (1967), *Essays in Labour History*, Macmillan.

BROUDY, H. S. (1962), 'To regain educational leadership', *Studies in Philosophy of Education*, no. 11., Spring.

BROUDY, H. S., SMITH, B. O., and BURNETT, J. R. (1965), *Democracy and Excellence in American Secondary Education*, Rand McNally.

BRUNER, J. S. (1964), *On Knowing: Essays for the Left Hand*, The Belknap Press of Harvard University Press.

BRUNER, J. S. (1965), *The Process of Education*, Harvard University Press.

BRUNER, J. S. (1966), *Toward a Theory of Instruction*, The Belknap Press of Harvard University Press.

BRUNER, J. S. (1972), *The Relevance of Education*, Allen & Unwin.

BRUNER, J. S., OLIVER, R. R., and GREENFIELD, P. M. (1966), *Studies in Cognitive Growth*, Wiley.

CARROLL, J. B. (1963), 'A model of school learning', *Teachers College Record*, 64, 723-33.

CHECKLAND, S. G. (1964), *The Rise of Industrial Society in England 1815-1885*, Longman.

CHOMSKY, N. (1966), *Cartesian Linguistics*, Harper & Row.

CICOUREL, A., and KITSUSE, J. (1963), *The Educational Decision-Makers*, Bobbs-Merrill.

CLARKE, P. (1973), 'An approach to sixth form general education through science including some aspects of the history and philosophy of science', unpublished M.A. dissertation, University of London, Institute of Education.

COLE, G. D. H. (1955), *Studies in Class Structure*, Routledge & Kegan Paul.

COLE, G. D. H., and POSTGATE, R. (1961), *The Common People 1746-1946*, Methuen (revised edition).

COX, C. B., and DYSON, A. E. (eds) (1969), *Fight for Education: A Black Paper*, Critical Quarterly Society.

DEARDEN, R. F. (1968), *The Philosophy of Primary Education*, Routledge & Kegan Paul.

DOUGLAS, J. D. (1971), *Understanding Everyday Life*, Routledge & Kegan Paul.

EISNER, E. W. (1969), 'Instructional and expressive education objectives: their formulation and use in curriculum', in Popham, W. J. *et al.* (eds), *Instructional Objectives*, AERA Monograph, no. 3, Rand McNally.

EISNER, E. W. (1971), *Confronting Curriculum Reform*, Little, Brown.

ELIOT, T. S. (1948), *Notes Towards a Definition of Culture*, Faber & Faber.

EVETTS, J. (1973), *The Sociology of Educational Ideas*, Routledge & Kegan Paul.

FILMER, P., *et al.* (1972), *New Directions in Sociological Theory*, Collier-Macmillan.

FORD, G. W., and PUGNO, L. (eds) (1964), *The Structure of Knowledge and the Curriculum*, Rand McNally.

FORD, J. (1969), *Social Class and the Comprehensive School*, Routledge & Kegan Paul.

FREIRE, P. (1971), *Pedagogy of the Oppressed*, Penguin.

GARDNER, K. (1968), 'The state of reading', in Smart, N. (ed.), *Crisis in the Classroom*, ch. 3, I.P.C.

GINSBERG, M. (1968), *Essays in Sociology and Social Philosophy*, Penguin.

GOLDBERG, M., and PASSOW, A. H. (1966), 'The affects of ability grouping', in Morgenstern, A. (ed.), *Grouping in the Elementary School*, Pitman.

GROOMBRIDGE, B. (1970), *The Londoner and his Library*, Research Institute for Consumer Affairs.

GURVITCH, G. (1971), *The Social Frameworks of Knowledge*, Blackwell.

HALBWACHS, M. (1958), *The Psychology of Social Class*, Heinemann.

HALSEY, A. H. (1972), E.P.A. Report, vol. I, HMSO.

HAMMOND, J. L., and HAMMOND, B. (1920), *The Town Labourer 1760-1832*, Longman.

HASS, G., WILES, K., and BONDI, J. (1970), *Readings in Curriculum*, Allyn & Bacon, 2nd ed.

HIRST, P. H. (1966), 'Educational theory', in Tibble (1966).

HIRST, P. H., and PETERS, R. S. (1970), *The Logic of Education*, Routledge & Kegan Paul.

HOGGART, R. (1960), *The Uses of Literacy*, Pelican.

HOGGART, R. (1970), *Speaking to Each Other*: vol. I *About Society*, vol. II *About Literature*, Chatto & Windus.

HOOPER, R. (ed.) (1971), *The Curriculum: Context, Design and Development*, Oliver and Boyd.

HUSEN, T. (1967), *International Study of Achievement in Mathematics*, 2 vols., Wiley.

ILLICH, I. (1973), 'The professions as a form of imperialism', *New Society*, 13 September.

JACKSON, B., and MARSDEN, D. (1962), *Education and the Working Class*, Routledge & Kegan Paul.

JAMES, L. (1963), *Fiction for the Working Man 1830-50*, Oxford University Press.

KEDDIE, N. (ed.) (1973), *Tinker, Tailor ... The Myth of Cultural Deprivation*, Penguin Education.

KERR, J. F. (ed.) (1968), *Changing the Curriculum*, University of London Press.

KLUCKHOHN, C. (1962), *Culture and Behaviour*, Free Press.

KOHLBERG, L. (1964), 'Development of moral character and ideology', in Hoffman, M. L. (ed.), *Review of Child Development Research*, vol. I, Russell Sage.

KORNHAUSER, A. (1965), *The Mental Health of the Industrial Worker*, Wiley.

KUHN, T. S. (1970a), *The Structure of Scientific Revolutions*, Chicago University Press, revised edn.

KUHN, T. S. (1970b), 'Reflections on my critics', in Lakatos & Musgrave (1970).

LAKATOS, I., and MUSGRAVE, A. (eds) (1970), *Criticism and the Growth of Knowledge*, Cambridge University Press.

LASLETT, P. (1965), *The World We Have Lost*, Methuen University Paperbacks.

LAWTON, D. (1969), 'The idea of an integrated curriculum', *University of London, Institute of Education Bulletin*.

LAWTON, D. (1973), *Social Change, Educational Theory and Curriculum Planning*, University of London Press.

BIBLIOGRAPHY

LEVIT, M. (ed.) (1971), *Curriculum (Readings in the Philosophy of Education)*, University of Illinois Press.

LUCKHAM, B. (1971), *The Library in Society*, Library Association.

MANN, M. (1973), *Consciousness and Action Among the Western Working Class*, Macmillan.

MANN, P. H. (1971), *Books, Buyers and Borrowers*, André Deutsch.

MANNHEIM, K. (1936), *Ideology and Utopia*, Routledge & Kegan Paul.

MANNHEIM, K. (1950), *Freedom, Power and Democratic Planning*, Routledge & Kegan Paul.

MAYER, K. B. (1955), *Class and Society*, Random House.

MCQUAIL, D. (1969), *Towards a Sociology of Mass Communications*, Collier-Macmillan.

MCQUAIL, D. (1970), 'The Audience for Television Plays', in Tunstall, (ed.) (1970).

MCQUAIL, D. (ed.) (1972), *Sociology of Mass Communications*, Penguin.

MIDWINTER, E. (1972), *Priority Education*, Penguin.

MIEL, A. (1963), 'Knowledge and the curriculum', in Frazier, A. (ed.), *New Insights and the Curriculum*, A.S.C.D. Washington, reprinted in Vandenberg (1969).

MOORHOUSE, H. F. (1973), 'The political incorporation of the British working class: an interpretation', *Sociology*, September, vol. 7, no. 3, pp. 341-59.

NISBET, J. D., and ENTWISTLE, N. J. (1969), *The Age of Transfer to Secondary Education*, University of London Press.

NISBET, R. A. (1967), *The Sociological Tradition*, Heinemann.

OSSOWSKA, M. (1971), *Social Determinants of Moral Ideas*, Routledge & Kegan Paul.

PARKINSON, M. (1970), *The Labour Party and the Organization of Secondary Education 1918-1965*, Routledge & Kegan Paul.

PETERS, R. S. (1966), *Ethics and Education*, Allen & Unwin.

PETERSON, A. D. C. (1960), *Arts and Science Sides in the Sixth Form*, Oxford University Dept. of Education.

PHENIX, P. H. (1962), 'The use of disciplines as curriculum content', *Educational Forum*, 26, reprinted in Levit (1971).

PHENIX, P. H. (1964), *The Realms of Meaning*, McGraw-Hill.

PIAGET, J. (1958), *The Development of Logical Thinking from Childhood to Adolescence*, Routledge & Kegan Paul.

PIAGET, J. (1972), *Psychology and Epistemology*, Penguin University Books.

PIVCEVIC, E. (1972), 'Can there be a phenomenological sociology?', *Sociology*, vol. 6, no. 3.

PLOWDEN REPORT (1967), *Children and Their Primary Schools*, HMSO.

POPPER, K. R. (1966), *The Open Society and Its Enemies*, Routledge & Kegan Paul (revised edn, 1966).

POPPER, K. R. (1970), 'Normal Science and its Dangers', in Lakatos and Musgrave (1970).

PRING, R. (1972), 'Knowledge out of control', *Education for Teaching*, Autumn.

RAWLS, J. (1972), *A Theory of Justice*, Oxford University Press.

ROBERTS, K. (1970), *Leisure*, Longman.

ROBINSOHN, S. B. (1969), 'A conceptual structure of curriculum development', Comparative Education Society in Europe Prague Conference 1969 (Mimeo).

RUSSELL, B. (1946), *History of Western Philosophy*, Unwin University Books.

SCHOOLS COUNCIL (1965), *Working Paper No. 2: Raising the School Leaving Age*.

SCHOOLS COUNCIL (1967), *Working Paper No. 12: The Educational Implications of Social and Economic Change*, HMSO.

SCHWAB, J. J. (1962), 'Disciplines and schools', in National Education Association, *The Scholars Look at the Schools*, Washington D.C.

SCHWAB, J. J. (1964), 'Structure of the disciplines: meaning and significances' in Ford & Pugno (1964).

SHAPIRO, H. L. (ed.) (1960), *Man, Culture and Society*, revised edn, Galaxy.

SILLITOE, K. K. (1969), *Planning for Leisure*, HMSO.

SMELSER, N. J. (1959), *Social Change in the Industrial Revolution: An Application of Theory to the Lancashire Cotton Industry 1770-1840*, Routledge & Kegan Paul.

STENHOUSE, L. (1967), *Culture and Education*, Nelson.

STENHOUSE, L. (1970), 'Some limitations of the use of objectives in curriculum research and planning', *Paedagogica Europaea*, vol. 6.

STENHOUSE, L. (1973), 'The humanities curriculum project', in Butcher, H. J., and Pont, H. B. (eds), *Educational Research in Britain 3*, University of London Press.

STEVENS, E. A. (1972), 'Library Members in Swindon: A survey', F.L.A. unpublished thesis.

STONES, E. (1970), *Readings in Educational Psychology, Learning and Teaching*, Methuen University Paperbacks.

TABA, H. (1962), *Curriculum Development Theory and Practice*, Harcourt, Brace & World.

TAWNEY, R. H. (1964), *Equality*, Unwin.

TAYLOR, L. C. (1971), *Resources for Learning*, Penguin.

THOMPSON, E. P. (1968), *The Making of the English Working Class*, Pelican.

TIBBLE, J. W. (1966), *The Study of Education*, Routledge & Kegan Paul.

TOULMIN, S. (1970), 'Does the distinction between normal and revolutionary science hold water?', in Lakatos & Musgrave (1970).

TUNSTALL, J. (ed.) (1970), *Media Sociology (A Reader)*, Constable.

TURNER, R. (1964), *The Social Context of Ambition*, Chandler.

TYKOCINER, J. T. (1964), 'Zetetics and areas of knowledge', in Phi Delta Kappa, *Education and the Structure of Knowledge*, Rand McNally.

TYLOR, E. B. (1871), *Primitive Culture*, Holt.

VANDENBERG, D. (ed.) (1969a), *Teaching and Learning*, University of Illinois Press.

VANDENBERG, D. (ed.) (1969b), *Theory of Knowledge and Problems of Education*, University of Illinois Press.

WEBB, R. K. (1955), *The British Working Class Reader (1790-1848)*, Allen & Unwin.

WEBER, M. (1952), *Essays in Sociology*, Gerth, H., and Mills, C. W. (eds), Routledge & Kegan Paul.

WHITE, J. (1973), *Towards a Compulsory Curriculum*, Routledge & Kegan Paul.

WHITFIELD, R. C. (ed.) (1971), *Disciplines of the Curriculum*, McGraw-Hill.

WILKINSON, R. (1964), *The Prefects*, Oxford University Press.

WILLIAMS, R. (1961), *The Long Revolution*, Pelican.

WILLIAMS, R. (1963), *Culture and Society 1780-1950*, revised edn, Pelican.

WILSON, A. B .(1963), 'Social stratification and academic achievement', in Passow, A. H. (ed.), *Education in Depressed Areas*, Teachers College, Columbia, New York.

WILSON, P. S. (1971), *Interest and Discipline in Education*, Routledge & Kegan Paul.

WILSON, T. P. (1971), 'Normative and Interpretive Paradigms in Sociology', in Douglas (1971).

WOLLHEIM, R. (1969), *Socialism and Culture* (Fabian Tract 331), Fabian Society.

YOUNG, M. F. D. (ed.) (1971), *Knowledge and Control: New Directions for the Sociology of Education*, Collier-Macmillan.

YOUNG, M., and ARMSTRONG, M. (1965), 'The flexible school', *Where*, supplement 5, Autumn 1965.